INNS *and* ADVENTURES
A History and Explorer's Guide

Vermont, New Hampshire and the Berkshires

Alison O'Leary
Michael J. Tougias

I

© 2015 Michael J. Tougias
ISBN 978-0-9913401-4-9 paperback
Book design/page layout, Jason Hart

To our parents,
Ed and Mavis O'Leary
and
Art and Jerri Tougias,
who inspired our love for the outdoors.

A Note to the Reader:

This is not your usual guidebook. It is part travelogue and part guidebook, sprinkled liberally with our passion for history and the environment.

The book is intended for active explorers, armchair travelers, and for those who simply like to read about the outdoors. Some of the chapters were written by Alison and Mike together, and some were written by each of us on solo trips. We do not claim that the inns featured in this book are better than those not in the book. Instead, we first chose an area that had extraordinary natural beauty and then researched what inn was located in the proximity and had a country setting. If we stayed at an inn that we did not enjoy, we simply omitted it from the book. The inns we do feature in the book met our criteria for being comfortable, quiet, and hosted by innkeepers that were knowledgeable and friendly.

If you plan on visiting a number of the areas we discuss we recommend you use the DeLorme Atlas and Gazetteer for the three states covered. For each chapter in the book we give you the corresponding pages in the Atlas. DeLorme does a fine job of detailing their topographic maps and we use them religiously for all our outdoor hobbies.

Whether you are a native New Englander or a visitor, we hope you enjoy our adventures, observations, and off-the-beaten-path destinations. Exploration can renew the spirit!

SOUTHERN VERMONT
(with Delorme Atlas Grid)

NORTHERN VERMONT
FROM SOUTH TO NORTH
(with Delorme Atlas Grid)

SOUTHERN & CENTRAL NH
(with Delorme Atlas Grid)

NORTHERN NH
(with Delorme Atlas Grid)

THE BERKSHIRES AND HILLTOWNS
(with Delorme Atlas Grid)

Vermont

SOUTHERN VERMONT

Waterfalls, Mills and Covered Bridges
(Dummerston, Newfane, Dover, Willmington)

Dummerston, Vermont is blessed with a number of unique rivers and brooks which all feed into the southeast flowing West River. Two of my favorites are Stickney Brook and the Rock River. The lower section of Stickney Brook which follows Pleasant Valley Road before meeting the West River at Route 30 has an incredible set of step stone falls that look like nature designed them specially for waterfall fanatics like myself. The brook tumbles down from Sunset Lake and cascades over a series of flat granite ledges, in some places falling like a perfect sheet. Photography buffs will be rewarded by sparkling clear water twinkling through dappled sunlight that filters through a hillside of maples and hemlocks. In some places the water comes down natural chutes and is directed into small, aqua colored pools.

If you hike along the stream you will notice giant granite blocks on the far side indicating that this was once a mill site. While the mill's purpose is unknown, maps label this particular spot as Old Jelly Mills Falls.

From Stickney Brook, river lovers can head northwest along the West River until you reach Williamsville Road on your left at the town line with Newfane. This is where the Rock River enters the West River. The Rock River is a popular swimming spot in the summer, and in the fall you can enjoy a nice riverside walk along a rough trail that follows the river upstream. (Parking is only allowed on the turnout at Route 30 rather than on Williamsville Road.)

On a warm September day I once snorkeled all the deep holes in the river expecting to see trout at the bottom of this mountain stream. Instead I was surprised to see smallmouth bass fining in the pools and one very large sucker which I actually caught in my hands before it wiggled free. In one shady spot in a pool about five feet deep there was a small snapping turtle sitting on the bottom, seemingly unconcerned by my presence just inches away. People usually expect to find snapping turtles in ponds and lakes, but they also inhabit large rivers, and as I found out first hand, small mountain rivers as well.

After my day of waterfall and river exploration, I headed west on Williamsville Road passing by the Williamsville covered bridge built in 1870 (118 feet long, Town Lattice), and through the sleepy hamlet of South Newfane, where gardeners may want to stop at the Olallie Daylily Garden, which features over 700 varieties of daylilies and many perennials. There is also a rock garden, diverse woodland and meadow plants, and over 40 Siberian iris cultivars.

Williamsville Road soon turns into Dover Road and passes out of New-fane and into Dover. Just before the road reaches Route 100 it passes through the northeast corner of Wilmington, Vermont.

Canoeists and kayakers will want to check out two nearby reservoirs, Har-riman Reservoir (aka Lake Whitingham) in Wilmington and Whitingham, and Somerset Reservoir in Somerset. Harriman Reservoir is the largest body of water completely within the state of Vermont. The entire shoreline, owned by U.S. Generating, is open to the public. If you don't have your own boat, canoe or kayak you can tour the lake with the Green Mountain Flagship Company on an hour and half boat ride.

Somerset Reservoir is more secluded than Harriman but is almost as large at a length of nine miles. This lake is for those who want quiet adventure as there are miles of hiking trails along the shoreline and no powerboats are per-mitted on the lake. You can, however, launch a canoe or kayak at the end of Somerset Road, and spend a day exploring the reservoirs nooks and crannies, hopefully spotting a loon or bald eagle that frequent the water.

Green Mountain Flagship Company: 802-464-2975

The Beauty of Jamaica

Vermont is known for its pristine rivers and wonderful hiking trails, and in the town of Jamaica the two complement each other. Jamaica State Park has one of New England's finest riverside trails on a two-and-a-half mile section of an old railroad bed that has been converted into a hiking and biking trail following the banks of the West River.

Besides the railroad bed, there are two other trails that hikers will love. One is a steep path to Hamilton Falls that cascades 125 feet onto smooth granite potholes. The other is the Overlook Trail leading to the summit of Little Ball Mountain where a series of vistas await from different ridges.

Activities for all seasons can be enjoyed at the park with hiking in the fall, snowshoeing and cross-country skiing in the winter, trout fishing in the spring, and swimming and hiking in the summer. The West River is also the site of white water canoe and kayak events in the spring and fall. History buffs will also enjoy the parks rich past. The railroad bed that is now a hiking trail was originally built in 1881, and trains ran from South Londonderry to Brattleboro daily. But because of the toll that river flooding took on the railroad, local residents began to refer to the railroad as "36 miles of trouble." More than once trains crossed a weakened section of track and crashed into the river.

Long before the railroad, the section of the West River flowing through the park was the scene of doom, when in 1748 Colonial soldiers were ambushed by French and Indians. Captain Eleazer Melvin was leading a contingent of eighteen men on a path along the river, and at the site of the current swimming hole in the park, they were ambushed. Total mayhem ensued, with some colonists running into the hills, some down the river and some upriver. Melvin wrote, "After I saw my own men retreat and being beset by the enemy with guns, hatchets and knives, several of them attempting to strike at me with their hatchets. Some threw their hatchets, one of which (or a bullet, I certainly cannot tell which) carried away my belt with it and my bullets…" Remarkably, Melvin was able to escape, but several of his men were not so lucky. The site was later referred to as the Salmon Hole Massacre.

Pike's Falls is located to the southwest of Jamaica Center and can be reached from town by driving approximately three or four miles on Pike's Falls Road. A trail leads downhill through the hemlocks until it emerges into the sunshine at Pike's Falls. Cascading water has cut a channel through the granite stone and tumbles into the a crystal clear pool, which is ten feet deep in spots. Be sure to bring your camera as the combination of water washing over the rocks surrounded by dark green hemlocks makes a great picture.

Jamaica State Park:
www.vtstateparks.com htm/jamaica.htm
802-874-4600

Rainbow Trout, Swimming Holes and the Bull Run Farm
(North Springfield and Reading)

There's nothing like having the whole day in front of you with nothing planned but endless possibilities. I was staying at the Bull Run Farm B&B, in North Springfield, Vermont, talking with innkeeper Cynthia Martin over coffee and breakfast. Cynthia was giving me tips on places to visit and I was forming a rough plan in my head that I'd take the old Subaru out and make a giant loop of the area.

"The only problem," I said, "is that when I take these rambles I have to stop at every stream, brook and river, just to see what the trout are doing."

"Why is that a problem?" asked Cynthia.

"Because sometimes I actually catch a fish, and then I forget all about the other places to see. Today will be different, I'm going to forget about the fishing and just let the road take me where it will."

Thirty minutes later I was in my waders, fishing rod in hand, wading up the Black River, picking my way between enormous boulders shaped by eons of water. So much for my resolve. But maybe I was meant to be on the river on this particular morning and this particular time, because on my very first cast I caught one of the largest rainbow trout I've ever tied into.

When the trout first hit I thought my lure was snagged, then the rainbow dove to the bottom of the river and I knew I was into a good fish. I talked myself through the next four minutes. *Don't blow it. Keep the rod tip up. Don't rush it. Just let him run. Let him tire. God he's big. Ok, start getting in position with the net.*

Normally the next words out of my mouth are unprintable because the fish somehow shakes free just as I lower my net. Today was different. I slipped the net beneath the trout, and scooped up an 18 inch rainbow with a vivid pink streak highlighting silver flanks.

Having caught a fish so early in the day was about the best thing that could have happened to me. Now I really would ramble, and it wouldn't matter if I caught another fish or not. Back at the car, I lay my atlas out on the hood and thought about where to head to next. Years ago I had heard about a great swimming hole on the North Branch of the Black River in Reading, so I set out to see if I could find it.

On my way to the swimming hole I saw a historic sign on Route 106, just a half mile south of the village of Felchville in Reading. There was a little turnout, and I parked my car, and walked up to two slate markers. Aha, I said to myself, I've been looking for these for years. They were the Susanna Johnson stones, set in the very spot where in 1754 Susanna gave birth to a baby girl. This was no ordinary birth, however, because at the time Susanna was a captive of Indians who had come down from Canada and attacked the few homes scattered around the Fort at Number Four in Charlestown, New Hampshire. It was only day two of Susanna's capture and forced march over the Green Mountains toward Lake Champlain when she gave birth. Fortunately, both mother and daughter not only survived the captivity, but eventually made it back to Colonies. (The markers are filled with curious etchings including tomahawks, spears, bow and arrows, and what appears to be an Indian standing and her baby lying down.)

When I reached the little village of Felchville, I turned west on South Reading Road, and after a bit of hunting around found the swimming hole known locally as Twenty Foot Hole for its depth. (Park about 1 mile up South Reading Road, and then it's a steep walk down through the woods to reach the river.) There are two beautiful, aqua-marine colored pools here that make a great spot for a picnic or a swim. Sunlight filters through giant hemlocks giving the chasm an enchanting feeling, so be sure to bring your camera.

After enjoying Twenty Foot Hole, I followed Route 44 eastward to Mount Ascutney State Park. I hiked on one of the mountains four trails but never did make it to the top of the mountain. Next time, I'll have to tackle the mountain first and do the fishing later if I want to enjoy Ascutney's breathtaking views of the both the Green and White Mountains as well as the Connecticut River Valley.

When I returned to Bull Run Farm B&B, it was late in the afternoon, and I sat by the pool with a beer letting my gaze drift over the meadow and the hills beyond. Cynthia and her husband Clint have lived in the handsome farmhouse for over 35 years, raising their family in this quiet corner of Vermont. When their children were grown, Cynthia opened the home as a B&B and it features three comfortable and affordable guest rooms. The atmosphere is casual and relaxing, and the inn is perfect for families with children because the farm still has two milk cows and several chickens. One recent guest had the honor of having a chicken lay an egg right in her hand! And those eggs ensure that the wonderful breakfasts of bacon and eggs are as fresh as can be.

The next day, I made the ten minute drive from Bull Farm into Springfield, where I walked about the town, especially enjoying The Vault, a gallery where local artists and crafts people exhibit their work. Next door I stopped into a charming little restaurant and munched on a sandwich while reading the paper. Springfield reminded me a little of Montpelier, because it's bigger than most town centers but too small to be city. Now that I think about it, Vermont really only has one city, Burlington, and maybe that's one of the reasons I love the state. There may be just one city (at least to my way of thinking), but so many little villages -- from Mosquitoville to Spoonerville -- that it would take a lifetime to pass through everyone. Maybe that should be my Vermont goal: keep rambling until I've seen every village and country crossroad in the state.

Bull Run Farm B&B:
www.bullrunfarm.net
802-886-8470

Over, Under and Through: Shrewsbury and Crisanver House Inn (Shrewsbury)

Walking the Appalachian Trail has its monotonous sections, where endless miles of dense forest is unbroken by a view, a river, or meadow. The section of trail through Shrewsbury, Vermont however has a nice diversion: a suspension footbridge spanning a scenic gorge, known as Clarendon Gorge. Here, the Mill River makes a right angle turn and becomes constricted by tall granite walls crowned by hemlocks and pines. A hiker can stand on the middle of the bridge and look below as the river thunders through the canyon, smoothing softer stone into twisting shapes. After crossing the suspension bridge I took a long walk on the Appalachian Trail, enjoying the shade of birch, maple, ash and pine.

The Gorge and the Appalachian Trail are on the border of Shrewsbury and Clarendon, and one of the area's more scenic country roads is just to the north in Clarendon. Look for the side road, called Airport Road off Route 103 that leads to the small airport. On this road is a boarded-up, rustic looking church, and it is here that you should turn down Gorge Road. This leads to a covered bridge built in the 1800's and the construction is Town Lattice Trust.

I parked my car on the side of the road and walked through the dark bridge, wishing there were a couple small windows inside to peer through and see an old mill by the side of the river. But when I reached the center of the bridge I had a pleasant surprise: a board had been removed from the side of the bridge and I could look clear up the river and admire the Kingsley Grist Mill perched above the water. A sign indicated that the mill was the last of a dozen mills that once dotted the river, serving to grind the grain.

Back at my car, I followed Gorge Road to the west as it hugged a ridge along the river. I especially liked this road because it was a dirt road with almost no homes on it. I'm convinced it's the many dirt roads that make Vermont special from other states, and once a town starts talking of paving them you can be sure the quiet, serene feeling of the old lane will be lost forever.

After parking on the side of Gorge Road, I bushwacked through the woods, heading toward the river. In the summer this is one of the swimming spots used by locals, but on this particular spring day it was just me and the river, and the river was really roaring. Water bounced over and around large boulders, making that rushing sound that only a mountain river can make, and which I've come to associate with happy times of tramping in the woods.

The gorge and the walk along the Mill River were just a couple of the interesting natural places I visited on my recent ramble through this section of Southern Vermont. Of course hiking and exploring are easy to do when you know that when nightfall comes you're going to be sleeping in complete comfort. For me, that meant staying at a hilltop B & B called the Crisanver House located on a beautiful dirt back road in Shrewsbury. This circa 1800's farmhouse has been totally renovated and innkeeper Michael Calotta explained to me that when he purchased the property in 1971 he wasn't even in the market for a B & B.

"My wife Carol and I were interested in a vacation home, but when the realtor showed us this property I had this feeling that this was the place we were looking for. The property was under contract to another buyer, but when that fell through we knew it was meant to be. Besides the historic farmhouse, we also purchased over a hundred surrounding acres of woods and fields," Michael says.

The Calottas' renovation and rebuilding of the inn was extensive, including the creation of a full basement (which is now a recreation room), removal of ceilings to expose antique beams, and all new bathrooms. Outside, a heated swimming pool was constructed, along with tennis courts and gardens. About the only thing not improved upon are the distant views over the rolling countryside. Shrewsbury, Clarendon, and the Crisanver House are worth the visit.

Crisanver House:
www.crisanver.com
800-492-8089

The entrance to Clarendon Gorge is just a five minute walk from at the parking area on Route 103 designated by a sign "Appalachian Trail."

Sledding Hills, Quiet Waters and Battlefields
Mountaintop Inn and Fox Creek Inn
(Chittendon and Hubbardton)

A great hill of green grass slopes away from the red umbrellas on the outdoor patio at Mountaintop Inn and Resort in Chittendon. It allows visitors to feel that they could take a few giant steps and be at the shore of the massive reservoir cupped by mountains below.

"There's one house, way over there, in the clouds," said Mountaintop marketing director Diane Dickerson, pointing to the east end of the water. "But the rest of the reservoir is surrounded by Green Mountain National Forest."

We spent a moment drinking in the unblemished view of spruce and water under blue skies, then Dickerson threw us a curve that was almost as alluring. "In winter, this is the best sledding hill anywhere," she said of the green slope at our feet. "The kids are out here all day, then the parents sometimes grab a sled after the kids are in bed, and they don't realize they're going to go a lot farther, a lot faster down the hill. They end up trudging back up here, having the time of their lives."

Sledding wasn't something that crossed our minds during our visit to the resort in summertime. Horseback riding, hiking, kayaking on the reservoir and shooting clay pigeons were all under consideration on this summer day, but sledding? Suddenly, we wanted to do that, too. And we might sometime in the future, because this is a year-round destination, turning its hiking and horseback riding trails into miles of groomed cross-country ski terrain in winter. And it's all just a few miles from Killington resort's downhill skiing as well.

The 350-acre resort packs in an astounding 90 weddings a year, owing to its beautiful backdrop, serene location and first-class facilities, but we focused on the activities that don't involve ceremony. Indeed, it was difficult to focus on just one or two possibilities, so upon arrival we divided and conquered: Mike checked out the kayaks on the quiet reservoir (of course looking for the giant walleye that are stocked there) and Alison hit the resort's state-of-the-art gym next to the pool. That night, as guests gathered for dinner outdoors on the patio, friends visited for a trip to the arcade and a late dessert of superb ice cream in the resort restaurant.

Our room was ski lodge perfection: log cabin quilts on the comfy beds, some of the best pillows ever, and a flat-screen television mounted on the

wall next to a heavy old wooden ski that made us wonder if our grandparents were much, much stronger than we would ever be. Just outside the wall of windows were a bed of hollyhocks and lilies framing a wonderful view of the reservoir.

In the end, clay pigeon shooting topped our list of activities to partake of here. Fortunately, we had a great teacher in lifelong Mountaintop employee Roger Hill, who said he has held every job here from leading trail rides to working in the kitchen. But it's obvious that teaching shooting is his niche.

"Put the butt of the gun here, and your cheek against the stock like this," he said, lifting the shotgun to eye level and nestling it into the hollow of his shoulder. Follow the clay from right to left, he coached, without taking your bead eye off the target.

We each loaded and emptied the double-barreled gun several times, trying to improve on our technique with Roger's patient assistance. We hit about a quarter of the bright-orange clays, trying to imitate the marksman's forward-leaning stance. But it was clear his smooth handling of the gun was result of many years of hunting and shooting, which we could never quite duplicate.

What changes has Roger seen over the years? "We're competing with electronic games," he said of getting kids – including his own – outdoors to participate in the sort of activities that the resort offers.

But, that said, Mountaintop is not giving up the battle. Dickerson says they're looking for a dogsled master to bring more winter thrills to their guests. "We had dogsled rides a few years ago and it was a huge hit. We'd like to bring that back."

Another option nearby that's quieter and more intimate than the lodge at Mountaintop is Fox Creek Inn just down the hill. Offering eight guest rooms with Jacuzzi tubs, fireplaces and a sumptuous breakfast in a cozy dining room, 100 years ago it was the wealthy Barstow family's summer home, welcoming the likes of Henry Ford and Thomas Edison.

It's no surprise this charming location has been a favorite getaway for decades as it's nestled by a rushing stream and surrounded by towering maples. Yet beyond the natural beauty of the area there's a strong community that takes care of their own.

Innkeeper Susan Smart and her husband, Bob, had traveled the world and dreamed of settling in a place like this to hosts other weary wanderers. They fell in love with the property and bought it with high hopes. Sadly, Bob passed away suddenly just a month later. But the community rallied around Susan. "They don't make empty promises and many helped," she says. "The inn provided the 'work therapy' I needed to get through the first months. Now I feel very at home here."

Both inns are great bases for exploring the area. For canoeists, kayakers and those in small boats the 721 acre Chittenden Reservoir is a nature lovers paradise because of the undeveloped shoreline and powerboat restrictions (15 horse power and a maximum speed of 5 miles per hour). The many coves and bays are perfect for exploring and for a swim on a hot summer's day. Besides the warm water species (largemouth bass, smallmouth bass, walleye) the reservoir is stocked with brook, rainbow and brown trout as well as those incredible leaping landlocked salmon. Depth of the lake reaches about 30 feet which gives these cold water species a place to stay cool in the heat of summer. (Guests at the Mountaintop have the use of several kayaks to choose from at the inn's private beach on the reservoir.)

If you paddle the reservoir be sure to bring binoculars because it's a good bet you will spot some kind of wildlife that makes its home in Vermont. Could be a loon, an otter, a merganser, or even a bear. Moose are sometimes seen here or in the marshes around Lefferts Pond, located at the southern end of the reservoir. This 49 acre pond is shallow, but offers superb birding and no motors of any kind are allowed on watercraft. Hiking trails begin near the pond and head north toward the reservoir.

For history lovers, a 40-minute drive to the Hubbardton Battlefield is well worth the effort. You can access it by going into Rutland and then heading west on Route 4 to exit 5 and then north on Frisbee Hill Road/East Hubbardton Road. (If you want to avoid the congestion of Rutland you can drive to Pittsford (one town west of Chittendon) and then proceed south on Route 3 and then west on Route 4 to exit 5.)

The battle fought at Hubbardton was the only battle of the Revolution that occurred entirely in modern day Vermont. Although not a large battle or as well known as say, Bunker Hill, it was an important one. The Green Mountain Boys fought a rear guard action on July 7, 1777 so that larger forces of American soldiers at Mount Independence and Fort Ticonderoga could escape the on-coming British Army.

The Patriots in Hubbardston held their ground long enough to slow the British, so that the American's could fight another day, which they did soon thereafter, defeating the British at Saratoga.

One of the great things about this battlefield is the setting: rolling fields cresting small hills with views. You can't help but stroll the crests of the mowed hills, walk alongside the stone walls, admire the mountains in all directions, and be thankful that the violence has been replaced by such beauty and peace.

Mountaintop Inn:
www.mountaintopinn.com;
802-483-2311

Fox Creek Inn:
www.foxcreekinn.com
802-483-6213

Letting Natural Curiosity Flow
Combes Family Inn and Lareau Farm Inn
(Ludlow, Waitsfield)

Thoreau wrote, "We are slow to realize water, the beauty and the magic of it." That observation might be true of adults, but children and teenagers seem to be drawn to water, especially rivers, and view them as a place of never-ending adventure.

My eleven-year-old son Brian and his friend Joey accompanied me on a Central Vermont ramble, where we explored the Mad River and Branch Brook. Instead of the boys sitting in front of a t.v. screen mesmerized by PlayStation or Nintendo we spent the weekend swimming, fishing and snorkeling in deep pools. The river brought out their natural curiosity where they used their mind's gift of imagination, learning about the natural world in a slow, unstructured way.

Of the many sections of river we explored, Buttermilk Falls on Branch Brook in Ludlow, Vermont, was one of our favorite spots. The headwaters of the brook are on Okemo Mountain where it first heads north then east, following Route 103 until it merges with the Black River. The waterfall is on Buttermilk Falls Road which is a side road off Route 103 just west of its junction with Route 100. Ice cold water plunges through a narrow gap in the granite rocks before spilling into an emerald pool. We took turns jumping from the rocks into the pool until the cold made our feet numb. The boys however, didn't want to leave, and they began hunting for crayfish and minnows in the shallows. That's when it hit me that if a child is given a chance to explore the natural world they can find endless ways to entertain themselves and learn a little bit in the process.

After a day on the river we went to Coolidge State Park in the evening where I was scheduled to give a lecture and slide presentation about the Connecticut River. I've given my presentations in a variety of places from elegant banquet halls to the basements of churches, but never in an open-air shelter. I wondered if this location would work, but the park rangers knew what they were doing, carrying a generator to the shelter to power my slide projector and making a roaring fire in the fireplace to add a touch of warmth on a cool night.

That night we had reservations at the Combes Family Inn, located on quiet country back road in Ludlow. Ruth and Bill Combes have restored this handsome farmhouse which has six guests rooms and an additional five guest rooms in an attached unit where pets are allowed. Brian, Joey and I stayed in a large room where the boys were excited to sleep in a bunk bed while I slept soundly in a room overlooking a rolling pasture.

For breakfast we ate about twenty of the Combes' tasty pancakes, and fueled ourselves for our second day of exploration. We headed north on Route 100 and made a short stop at Gifford Woods State Park that features a virgin stand of towering hardwoods. Usually such old growth forests are deep in the woods on the side of steep ravines, but these trees are next to Route 100, somehow escaping the ax and bulldozers. Don't expect redwood size trees if you go, but nevertheless I found the 100 foot tall maples quite impressive.

After our walk through the old growth we drove on to Waitsfield, heading directly to one of my favorite swimming holes on the Mad River. There, a twenty-five foot ledge of granite rises above a fifteen-foot deep pool, and like the day before we made several jumps from the rock into the gin-clear water. Best of all, we didn't have to do any more driving when we were done swimming, because we were staying right across the street at the Lareau Farm Country Inn. Our hostess Susan Easley not only makes guests comfortable and prepares hearty breakfasts, but she also keeps animals that were a big hit with the boys. Adjacent to the inn is American Flatbread, a restaurant that makes delicious all natural pizza baked in a primitive wood-fired oven.

Later that evening the boys and I went trout fishing in the river and Joey caught his first brook trout from its lair under a tangle of roots. We also tried fishing at the big pool we had earlier swam in. Although we did not catch anything, Joey took an unintentional swim when he slipped on a rock. He then figured that since he was wet he might as well jump of the big ledge. That's when the boys learned another lesson about rivers: it's not a good idea to go swimming with long pants and a sweatshirt on, unless you want to *walk* on the bottom of the fifteen-foot deep pool. Despite the weight of the wet clothing Joey did make it to shore without my help, and then he continued fishing as if nothing happened.

I guess that makes him a true outdoorsman with a real-life adventure rather than a simulated one on a video game.

Coolidge State Park has 35 lean-tos and 25 tent and trailer sites. Telephone numbers are: 1-802-672-3512 in summer, and 1-800-299-3071 from January to May. The park is close to the Calvin Coolidge Historic Site which is a re-created village from President Coolidge day.

This is one of the most beautiful historic sites in New England.

The Combes Family Inn:
www.combesfamilyinn.com
800-822-8799

The Lareau Farm Country Inn:
www.lareaufarminn.com
800-833-0766

Gifford Woods State Park has several well spaced campsites.
Call 802-775-5354 in the summer or 802-866-2434 in the winter.

Exploring the History and Beauty of Lake Champlain
Whitford House Inn (Fort Ticonderoga, NY)

From the cliff-top perch at Mount Defiance in Ticonderoga, New York, I could see Lake Champlain stretching north and south in a ribbon of blue set between the green rolling hills of Vermont and New York. A cool September breeze refreshed me after the one mile walk up the access road. It's hard to imagine a more peaceful scene, but in the 1700s the lake was the site of one battle after another during both the French and Indian Wars and the American Revolution.

Four cannons point northward from the summit of Mount Defiance, aiming directly at Fort Ticonderoga which can be seen in the distance. From this lofty vantage point it's easy to see why Ticonderoga was such a strategic location. The hill where the fort was built overlooks the narrows of Lake Champlain and it would be hard for any boats to slip by without notice. And just below the fort is the mouth of the La Chute River which connects Champlain to Lake George, another critical link in the colonial travel route between Montreal and Albany. Military leaders from Montcalm to Abercrombie recognized that whoever controlled the narrow passage at Ticonderoga controlled military transport into the heart of the country. (The name Ticonderoga is from the Iroquois, meaning "place between the waters.")

After viewing Lake Ticonderoga from the mountain, it was time to head down and actually tour the fort itself. The first thing that impressed me about the fort is that the wooded acres around it have been protected, allowing the visitor to experience the setting much as it might have been 200 years ago. (There's nothing worse than visiting an important historic site only to find it encircled by condos, malls and traffic. Fort Ticonderoga is the opposite, the entrance road passes through dark woods and fields where some of the trenches dug by the French can still be seen.)

Once inside the fort, I had a sense of what it must have been like to defend it. You can stand at the thick stone walls where row upon row of cannon overlook the lake and imagine this was a howling wilderness with the fort at the French's southernmost outpost. The French first began construction of the fort in 1755, and built it in such a way to protect the southern part of the lake below the fort, because that would be the direction any British attack would come from.

Just a few miles to the north on Lake Champlain, at another constriction in the lake, is the fort at Crown Point. Built by the French in 1737 and called Fort St. Frederic, it housed 100 men. A small settlement sprang up around the fort, making it the first European community in the southern Champlain Valley. French patrols from the fort attacked the English and colonists at such locations as Deerfield Massachusetts and Fort William Henry at Lake George.

The British mounted four campaigns to take Fort St. Frederic, and finally succeeded in 1759. British soldiers and engineers then greatly expanded the fort with three redoubts, a series of blockhouses and interconnecting roads. Large stone blocks were used for the barracks, and rampart walls were 30 feet thick and 40 feet high, made of earth piled between log cribs. The ramparts were the main outer wall to protect the interior from artillery fire and to elevated defenders to a commanding position from which to fire on the enemy. The earth dug to build the ramparts was taken directly from the ground in front of the fort, leaving ditches that would slow down the enemy.

The fort changed hands again in 1775 when the rebellious colonists captured it. Cannons taken from the British were hauled all the way to Boston by Colonel Henry Knox's men, forcing the Redcoats out of the city. The Americans didn't hold the fort for too long, evacuating when General Burgoyne's army forced them out.

Today the ramparts, ditches and stone barracks can still be seen, and there is a visitor's center with displays. Views from the fort are magnificent. You can stand atop the ramparts and look northward to purple mountains rising above the blue waters and whitecaps of Lake Champlain. As a photography buff, I especially loved this scene: the fort's gray stonework in the foreground and nature's grandeur beyond.

For lodging near the fort, I chose Whitford House, a B&B located in Vergennes, Vermont. The moment I pulled into the driveway I said to myself, "now this is a real country inn." A wrap-around porch, stone walls, rock gardens and even a swing from a giant maple surrounded the restored 1790s home. Rolling fields stretch toward Lake Champlain and beyond rise the hills of the Adirondack Mountains. Inside, the inn was just as nice with a well-stocked library, wood-burning fireplaces and comfortable guestrooms.

Owner Barbara Carson, a native Californian, explained that she and her husband bought the house in 1988 after searching for a place with just the right views. They thought they would just use it as a summer house, but after staying in the winter they decided to stay here permanently. So many friends came to visit that the Carsons decided to open the house as a B&B so others could enjoy the peace of the Vermont countryside.

Barbara and I talked in the morning over breakfast, and I explained how I had a cabin in Northern Vermont and that I'd recently heard about a sighting of a mountain lion. Barbara then told me a fascinating story. "One of our helpers, a girl that grew up here, came to us out of breath and said, 'Look in the field, I think there's a mountain lion!' Four of us were sitting on the deck and we looked down to the field and there it was, the most magnificent creature. It was unmistakable with its long tail, standing stock still. The cougar turned, looked at us, then slowly stalked off. This all happened right in the middle of the afternoon."

When I drove home that afternoon I thought about how man had forever altered the wilderness around Lake Champlain since the days of the French and Indian Wars and the Revolution. But the story about the mountain lion gave me a sense of hope that maybe we still have time to protect these green forests before it's too late.

Fort Ticonderoga:
www.fortticonderoga.org
518-585-2821
Crown Point State Historic Site:
www.nysparks.com
518-597-4666

Whitford House:
www.whitfordhouseinn.com
802-758-2704

Bears and Blueberries at the Blueberry Hill Inn
(Goshen, Salisbury)

At first I thought the bear cub crossing the road was a black lab, but there was no mistaking it when stopped and turned its large furry head toward me. The cub seemed as uncertain as I did as to who should make the next move. It hesitated in the middle of the road for a few seconds before wheeling around and returning to the side from which it came. It then quickly climbed ten feet up a large white pine.

I fumbled in my backpack for my camera, and took a picture from where I stood. But from a distance of thirty feet, the picture was not a good one. What to do? Prior to this encounter I'd only seen two bear in the woods, and both were adults. A photo of this cub had the potential to be one of my best pictures yet, but I'd have to move a few feet closer for a better shot. I reasoned the cub had returned to the side of the road its mother was on. I moved closer but stayed on the opposite side of the country lane, searching the woods with my eyes for something big and black.

The cub held its position on the trunk of the tree, eyeing me warily. If the mother was nearby, as I'm certain she was, she was holding her position back in the woods, unseen. I was now diagonally across from the bear cub, with nothing but the roadway separating us. I raised my camera and took three great shots before my roll of film reached its end. I lowered the camera and started to take of my backpack to get film, when a thought went through my thick head, sending a chill up my spine.

The cub was probably crossing the road because it was following its mother--which meant the mother bear might be directly *behind* me. I felt like a kid who thinks something is under his bed but is afraid to look. I turned my head ever so slowly without moving the rest of my body, and scanned the dark hemlocks, which were just five feet away. They were in shadow, and the woods so thick there could have been two bears watching me and I wouldn't know.

Now I prayed the cub wouldn't let out a bawl, because all I could think of was a charging mother bear, intent on grabbing the human that forced its cub up a tree. Not wanting to press my luck I moved up the road, the way I'd come. When I looked back, the cub had scrambled down the tree and disappeared into the forest.

Such are the sights and adventures one might see in Vermont. I was glad I wasn't camping that night, not only because it started to pour but because the image of an angry mother bear carrying off a bespectacled photographer wouldn't leave my head. Thankfully, I had lodging at the Blueberry Hill Inn in Goshen, Vermont, where I could enjoy thousands of wild, wooded acres in the Green Mountain National Forest, but sleep in a comfy inn.

Upon arrival, the office manager gave me brief tour of the restored 1813 farmhouse, pointing out a wood-fired sauna out back beyond a pond. I hadn't taken a sauna in many years, but I thought it might be the perfect form of relaxation after the excitement of seeing the bear cub. Who knows, maybe it would have therapeutic powers like the Native American sweat lodge.

After my sauna, my leg muscles felt like spaghetti, so I took a short walk. Even in a light drizzle I could appreciate the beauty of the grounds of the inn. There were all manner of flowers growing, and a rushing brook tumbled out of the mountains by the side of the pond.

That night I joined other guests around a large table in the dining room and enjoyed a fantastic dinner by Chef Tim Cheevers. I learned that other guests also chose the inn because of the great hiking on the 120 acre property and the thousands of acres in the adjacent Green Mountain National Forest. I also discovered that innkeeper Tony Clark formed the Moosalamoo Association, a land trust partnership that has helped to preserve the natural beauty of this region.

In the morning I hiked up nearby Rattlesnake Point. At the summit I enjoyed sweeping views to the south, looking down on Lake Dunmore and Silver Lake in the foreground and the purple-green mountains beyond. On the way off the mountain I stopped to gather some succulent blueberries which made me think the bear cub would have also liked this spot.

Blueberry Hill Inn:
www.blueberryhill.com
802-247-6735

The Place that Inspired Robert Frost
Whitford House Inn
(Ripton and Addison)

If you walk the back roads of Ripton, Vermont it's easy to understand where Robert Frost got his inspiration. A sublime kind of poetry is in the trees, the hills, and the hardscrabble farms that dot the countryside in this Central Vermont town. Frost wrote about the road not taken, but here I want to take them all, not missing a vista or a hidden trout stream.

For 24 summers Frost lived in Ripton, writing his poetry and reading his works at the Bread Loaf campus of Middlebury College. Frost stayed at the Homer Noble Farm and wrote in a cabin nearby. Neither are easy to find. Both the farm and the cabin are situated off Route 125 and are not visible from the main road. Visitors should first locate the Bread Loaf Campus with its distinctive yellow buildings and then head west on Route 125 to the Robert Frost Wayside where picnic tables stand in a shady pine grove. Just a quarter mile east is an unmarked lane that leads to the Noble Farm and Frost's cabin. The setting is secluded and both buildings are surrounded by a combination of fields and handsome maple trees – it might inspire you to do some writing of your own.

On my visit, I first explored area around Frost's cabin then later drove east on Route 125, stopping at Middlebury Gap, the road's highest elevation at 2,144 feet where I took a short hike on the Long Trail heading south to the Robert Frost Lookout. Climbing on this trail that runs in a north-south direction through central Vermont, always makes me wish I had the time to do the whole thing, not stopping until the Canadian border. It may be a few years before that happens, but it sure would be a good challenge no matter how old I am.

Later I drove through Middlebury and headed west toward Addison. The landscape changes dramatically from the forested mountainous terrain of Ripton to the cornfields of Addison that roll gentle waves toward Lake Champlain. It's this diversity within a half hour drive that makes me love this region of Vermont.

At Willow Point by the mouth of Dead Creek on Lake Champlain I watched ten wild turkey feeding by the roadside. When I stepped out of my car the birds surprised me by flying rather than running for cover. They were much more graceful than the fat barnyard domesticated turkeys, and I understood why Benjamin Franklin wanted to make the turkey, rather than the eagle, our national symbol.

I spent the night at the Whitford House B & B in Vergennes, where Barbara and Bruce Carson always make me feel like one of the family. I love the dirt roads that wind past their inn, and the next morning I walked them, enjoying the crunch of dirt and gravel underfoot. Walking rather than driving allows you to see things you would otherwise miss from the car. A couple miles into my walk I passed a home with weathered boards devoid of paint which appeared abandoned. The roof of the home and roof of the attached barn were sagging into one another, and I wondered how many more winters they would withstand. What stories that home could tell.

As I completed my walk it occurred to me that some people would view dirt roads as needing "improvement" to allow cars to travel faster. But improvement means I would have never spotted the abandoned home nor enjoyed the flight of the wild turkeys.

If there's a road near your home that is still dirt and gravel, fight to leave it that way. Slow can be beautiful.

The Whitford House:
www.whitfordhouseinn.com
800-746-2704

Snorkeling For Trout, Floating Bridges and The Green Trails Inn
(Royalton, Randolph, Brookfield, Williamstown)

Central Vermont's rolling hills and back roads tug at your heart, beckon you to slow down and *explore* rather than drive, to feel rather than just see. Around each bend and up each crest of a hill the scenery seems to get better and better, with enough beauty to make the heart sing.

One such road is Route 14. By exiting Interstate 89 at the town of Sharon, you can follow this country lane northwest along the White River, a clear, swift flowing waterway where the trout grow large. I've caught my share of trout here, but the biggest one I ever saw was up close and personal. With mask and snorkel I once jumped in the river and swam to the base of a small falls. Thousands of white bubbles swirled around me, like a winter blizzard, and at the edge of pounding current were a number of small trout. I dove down to the bottom of the pool, and that's where I saw the big rainbow trout. It had wedged itself between two rocks, letting the current carry its food while it stayed protected. Rather than dart away, the trout stayed there, letting me look for as long as I could hold my breath, as if knowing it had nothing to fear.

On this trip I neither fished nor swam, content to merely cruise up and down the hills. I stopped in South Royalton, admiring the large village green while eating lunch beneath a massive maple. The most handsome building by the side of the common was the 1850 South Royalton House. Later I took a long walk up one of the side roads, letting all my senses take in the mountains--the earthy smell of ferns, the green hills so easy on the eyes, and the sound of a ruffed grouse, its muted drum roll carried on the breeze.

After Royalton I poked northward, passing through Randolph and then turning off Route 14 and onto Route 66 which leads into the little hamlet of Brookfield. A few homes are clustered around a crossroads, where one of man's stranger creations lies. A floating bridge spans Sunset Lake; the longest one east of the Mississippi, and perhaps the only one anywhere in the country that still supports regular traffic.

Directly across from the bridge is the Green Trails Inn, my destination for the night. Now owned by cookbook author Jane Doerfer, it's known for dining on local products, fantastic beds, vintage linens and as a special place where guests can unwind with a good book and relax. Nature lovers will appreciate the many activities available just outside the front door such as hiking, fishing, swimming, bicycling and canoeing. During the winter there is cross country skiing on over 30 kilometers of trails that wind through forest of hemlock, spruce, maple and beech.

The Inn was built in the 1830's and one building dates even further back, to 1790. Each room is unique in its character and all are comfortably elegant. Large groups can be accommodated comfortably as well.

The next morning I explored Allis State Park, just west of the floating bridge. Like so much of New England the forest in the park is second growth--the land had been cleared for agriculture in the 1700's. Signs of the past, such as old stone walls and an apple tree struggling for light beneath the native maples and birch, offer clues of the settlers' earlier presence. From the top of a fire tower one can see Mount Mansfield and Camels Hump to the north, Killington and Ascutney to the south, and the White Mountains of New Hampshire to the east.

Later I found my way back to Route 14, heading north towards my little cabin in the hills. The openness of the road gradually was replaced by steep wooded mountains crowding the valley. This was the Williamstown Gap, where patches of snow can often be seen even as late as May. It's rugged, isolated country, where nature seems harsh.

But still there was beauty. A single white birch amidst the dark green spruce stood alone, catching my eye. Yes, recognizing beauty just may be the most important step to a more spiritual life, a life connected to the earth itself.

The Green Trails Inn:
greentrailsinn.com
802-276-3412

The Hills North of Montpelier
(Montpelier, Calais, Cabot)

Every spring I get multiple fevers: fishing fever, gardening fever, and hiking fever. But none of these compare to the power of cabin fever. Not the kind of cabin fever where you want to escape from the cabin; no, mine is just the opposite -- I can't wait to get to my cabin.

Anyone who has ever owned a summer place knows the anticipation and joy of the first visit in the springtime to the old cabin, or "camp" as they're called in Vermont. Opening camp is a ritual one grows to love, a symbolic way of affirming the cycles of one's life.

Last spring I arrived in Montpelier, just south of my cabin, early in the morning, and since I had the whole weekend, decided to explore some gravel roads I'd never been down before. First I loaded up with provisions at the Country Store in Montpelier: Ben and Jerry's Ice Cream, imported beer, a cigar, and a huge sandwich for lunch. Before leaving Montpelier, the smallest state capital in the Union, I stopped at the Vermont Historical Society Museum. I wanted to see something I'd been thinking a lot about.

In the little museum is a 182-pound cougar, shot in the mid 1800's. It is said to be the last mountain lion in New England. But that was before the summer of 1994, when mountain lions were seen and officially confirmed as being back in our northern forests. (Scat was located, analyzed, and found to contain the hairs from a mountain lion; consistent with all cat's habit of licking their fur clean.) The museum also housed period costumes, tools, furnishings, and curiosities, but it's the cougar or catamount that steals the show, and I wondered if I'd ever see one in the wild.

From Montpelier I took Main Street north, stopping at Morse Farm with its little sugar house and miniature sugaring museum. Fresh produce, from asparagus in the spring to apples in the fall will lure you into the large farm store, where you may meet Harry "Burr" Morse Jr., who runs the farm with his family. Harry always has a story, and he is truly a creative individual--come back in the fall to see the 16 foot cornucopia he makes.

Main Street turns into County Road, and descends into the little hamlet of Maple Four Corners. By turning right here, you will be on a dirt road, one of several thousand that criss-cross the state, and to my way of thinking offer the best way to see the real Vermont. Follow this road two miles, past the old Calais Town Hall (1866) resting alone in a meadow, until you reach the end of the road, where you should turn left. By staying on this road you will pass first through farmland, then the little village of North Calais, and finally up a hill that offers a sweeping view of Mirror Lake. A mile farther brings you to a ridge above South Woodbury, where the Congregational Church can be seen below. If you feel like you've been here before, it's probably because the view looking down on the church appears in many postcards of Vermont.

When I reached Route 14 I headed north then turned east, following the signs for Cabot along another dirt road. The center of Cabot looked like it was frozen in time. The Cabot United Church overlooks a quiet village green, and for the few minutes I walked about town only a couple cars passed. Just south of the green is the Cabot Creamery, where tours are given of the cheese-making operation and a retail store sells all sorts of Vermont made dairy products.

To the east of town is Cabot Plains, a hilltop community that has a character all its own. A one room school house rests in the middle of a pasture, and nearby is a covered bridge, looking out of place spanning a small pond in a field. Cabot Plains Cemetery is perched high atop a hill, surrounded by a white fence and an arched entranceway. Some of the most stunning views in the region are just down the dirt road leading southward from the cemetery--but be warned; beauty like this will have you dreaming of moving up north.

And now I'm back at the cabin, typing this story on my little porch. Rolling hills stretch out before me, purple under a threatening sky. A cold front has moved in, and within the span of an hour I go from typing in a T-shirt to a sweater and then finally a down-filled jacket. My cabin will be cold tonight. I haven't gotten around to putting a wood stove in, although it's been on the "to do" list for five years. The problem is that every time I come up to the north country the woods, streams and pond call out to me, and off I go, never completing the projects planned each winter.

My cabin is not for everyone. There is no plumbing, a couple mice always seem to have taken up residence, and it's a four-hour drive from home. But oh, what tranquility. Visiting is an adventure in contentment. That's what's been bringing me back for 30 years.

Morse Farm:
www.morsefarm.com

The Upper Connecticut River:
McIndoe Falls Inn, a Hidden Spring and Alfred Hitchcock
(Northeast Kingdom)

Gloria LaBorie, innkeeper at the McIndoe Falls Inn, must have been able to read my mind. I was traveling north along the Connecticut River and planned on visiting three or four really out-of-the-way destinations in Vermont's Northeast Kingdom. One of the places was about an hour north of McIndoe Falls, in a little town called Brunswick, where five unusual springs flow out a hill and into the Connecticut River.

When I arrived at the Inn, Gloria and I chatted for a couple minutes and then she surprised me by saying, "you should visit the Indian Springs way up on the Connecticut River, in Brunswick."

I said, "Wow, I have an atlas in my car and it's open to the page on Brunswick with the location of the springs circled. You're a mind-reader!"

Besides Gloria's intuition, her inn keeping skills are first rate, because the McIndoe Falls Inn is the perfect setting for relaxation. All eight guest rooms are filled with antiques and each have feather beds. Breakfasts are made from organic produce and the wheat Gloria uses is ground fresh daily for use in her homemade breads and pancakes. Gloria also might hold the record for the longest run of inn keeping with her 40-plus years of owning and managing the inn. "Why stop doing what you love?" she said.

The outside of the inn is quite distinctive because it has four giant white columns that extend from the front of the two story home to the roof in a Greek revival style. A short walk across the street is the Connecticut River. On the downstream side of the Mcindoe Dam it's possible to walk the shoreline and discover giant pieces of driftwood scattered about, some with unique shapes.

After my night's stay at the inn, I headed north to find the Indian Springs, and also see what other unusual destinations I could find. My first stop was St. Johnsbury, home of the fascinating Fairbanks Museum and Planetarium. There's something there for everyone, including the largest natural science collection in Northern New England and Vermont's only public planetarium. My vote for the strangest exhibit in the museum goes to the portraits of American presidents made out of bugs!

From St. Johnsbury I drove northeastward into Victory Bog, where a single dirt road parallels Moose River and takes you through the heart of the bog. The road passes by open meadows, the rapids of the river, wetlands, and woods of maple, hemlock and fir. I stopped to read the words on a plaque imbedded in a boulder, which was in memory of Fred Mold who helped to preserve the bog. The message was a good one: "Where he met a stranger, there he left a friend."

Victory Bog is a good place to see moose, and, with a little luck, maybe even a bear. Deer are also abundant, and the state record, a 269 pounder with an enormous rack, was shot nearby. When you exit the north end of the bog be on the lookout for Alfred Hitchcock. That's right, a wooden cut-out of old Alfred is propped by the side of the road in Granby, adding to the isolation and mystery of the bog and the miles of unbroken wilderness.

Also in Granby on Porrel Hill Road is a lonesome gravesite. Buried at the spot are two of Major Robert Rogers Rangers. When Rogers and his men attacked the Indians of St. Francis, Canada, during the final two years of the French and Indian War, they were victorious. The victory of destroying the Indian village, however, was short lived, because the Rangers had a terrible time getting out of enemy country and back to the colonies. A local historian told me that the two men who lie beneath this gravesite, died just after they shot a moose. The men were dressing the moose when they were attacked by wolves and killed. (Maybe old Alfred was on my mind, but it occurred to me that this bizarre and terrifying event seemed like it could have been in an Alfred Hitchcock movie.)

My final stop was Brunswick and the springs. I parked at the Town House and walked on the trail for about twenty minutes. When I spotted some cement steps in the woods not far from the Connecticut River, I knew I had the place. Flowing out of the hillside and cascading down to the river, were the springs. Each spring is said to have a mineral content different than the next.

While I was there I met two other hikers, and one of the two had formerly lived in Brunswick, and he knew the story of the springs. "We were always told they were cursed. The Indians used to visit them, but then the whiteman came and drove out the natives. Two or three hotels were built on this site, and all of them burned down. The legend is that the Indians cursed anyone who tried to use the springs for profit." The man I met also added that this location had also seen two suicides. Again, I thought of old Alfred Hitchcock. I wondered if he'd ever visited the springs.

MacIndoe Falls Inn:
www.macindoefallsinn.com
802-633-2240

Beautiful Boondoggle Leads to Forgotten Hilltops
(Northeast Kingdom, Peacham and Cabot)

The Bayley-Hazen Road was built during the Revolution in hopes that it would be used by Colonial troops for an attack on Canada. The road was never completed, but much of its path is now on a network of dirt roads that head in a northwest direction through Vermont's Northeast Kingdom.

On a recent outing I picked up the Bayley-Hazen Road in Peacham and followed the Danville Road north, passing stately farmhouses and traveling over rolling hills. Follow the Danville Road for 1.7 miles and then bear left at a fork. A sign signals that this is the Bayley-Hazen Road, although my atlas called this dirt road Joe's Pond Road. This dirt lane hugs the side of ridge and is lined by giant sugar maples. Most of the surrounding acres are wooded, so be on the lookout for deer, moose, and maybe, with a little luck, a bear.

It's almost beyond comprehension that the builders of the Bayley-Hazen Road carved it out of the woods using nothing more than axes and oxen. Backbreaking work to say the least, and futile work as well, because the road project was abandoned when Colonial leaders realized the British might use this same road to come south and attack the Colonies. But I'm glad the road was constructed, and I refer to it as a "Beautiful Boondoggle" because it takes you through some of the best countryside Vermont has to offer.

The original Bayely-Hazen Road veered off from the road you are on after three miles and went in a more northeasterly direction just before the town line of Peacham and Danville. Unfortunately the original road is entirely overgrown, so you must pick it back up again in Cabot. That's easy to do, however, by simply following the dirt road we are traveling to Route 2 (about four and a half miles). When you reach Route 2 head west, paralleling the shores of Joe's Pond. Go a short distance and then bear right on West Shore Road, just after the state boat launch.

West Shore Road turns into Cabot Plains Road, and you should proceed 1.8 miles and bear left, staying on Cabot Plains Road. In half a mile you will pass a little red building that was the former Cabot Plains School, built in 1929. Continue traveling one mile to a T-intersection. This is where it's best to park your car and stretch your legs. If you turn left and walk half a mile on Dubray Road, you will arrive at an open area with some incredible views, and if you turn right you can visit the Cabot Plains Cemetery. The Cemetery is on a windswept hill, and is surrounded by a white fence and arched entrance.

Across the street is a strange site; a covered bridge out in the middle of a field that spans a pond that is no more than 100 feet by 50 feet. The bridge is dedicated to A.M. Foster (1830-1914) who invented the Foster Sap Spout.

Beyond the Cemetery and Covered Bridge is a little white building constructed in 1863 which once served as a one room school house. Across the street from the schoolhouse is a dirt road with a sign warning you that the road is not well maintained. This road is part of the original Bayley-Hazen Road, and although it's a bit bumpy, don't let that deter you. This road would be especially pleasant to walk on an autumn day, because it is lined by maples and probably has no more than one car per hour using it. This lane is appropriately called the Bayley-Hazen Road, and it runs for about a mile before it reaches Route 215. At its end is a stone marker erected to the first settlers in the region. It reads:

In memory of early settlers buried near this site on the Bayley-Hazen Military Road. Nathaniel West died 1786, crushed by a birch log while helping Benjamin Webster clear his land.

God my redeemer lives
And ever from the skies
Looks down and watches my dust
Till he shall bid it rise.

This marker and the little cemetery made me pause and think. My thoughts were this—enjoy the beauty of today because we are not promised tomorrow. And so I pushed on to my cabin and spent the afternoon swimming on the pond, enjoying one of the last sultry days of the summer.

When Possessions Slow Us Down
Hiking Stowe Pinnacle (Stowe)

The topographical map indicated the summit was 2600 feet and the trail was only one and a half miles. How hard could that be?

It was winter in Stowe, Vermont and I had set out to climb Stowe Pinnacle. I figured I'd be up and down the mountain in less than an hour and half and could later cross country ski on the Stowe Recreation Trail. I was wrong on both counts.

A light, dry snow was falling when I began the hike. Mine was the only car in the parking lot and I had the woods to myself. The trail began with a gradual ascent, passing through spruce, hemlock and stunted maples. Eight of nine inches of snow blanketed the forest, obliterating the rough edges, giving the woods a smooth and clean appearance. I had a backpack with the essentials of water, compass and other odds and ends, and I was dressed in several layers of clothing because the temperature was in the teens.

About a half mile up the trail its steepness increased considerably, and I found myself panting and sweating from the exertion. Off came my jacket. Another quarter mile up the trail I stopped for a water break and off came my sweater. A few more minutes and I was still heating up so I took my flannel shirt off. Now I was down to just a polypropylene turtleneck. It was the first time I had worn this turtleneck, and the polypropylene was living up to its promise of wicking away the perspiration from my body, and I made a mental note to wear it more often when hiking.

An hour had gone by and the summit was still not visible. I wondered if I should turn back, considering that I was now almost crawling up the slope. The trail was icy in spots and it required me to use my hands to grip various rocks and trees in order to scale the tricky spots.

My thigh muscles were burning and my backpack felt extra heavy. I'm 50 years old and in good shape, but I certainly didn't feel it. A raven sat near the top of a spruce and seemed to mock me. *"Auk, auk, auk"* it called out. Translation: wimp, wimp, wimp. With its call echoing down the mountain, I sat down on a rock and took a long drink from my water bottle and let my wind come back.

I decided to take a look inside my backpack, wondering why it felt so heavy. Over the years I had accumulated various items that I'd stuffed into the pack, thinking someday I just might need them. Here is what I found inside the pack: my camera, six rolls of film, telephoto lens, a book to identify wild plants, a book to identify animal tracks, matches, compass, toilet paper, four pocket knives, six pens, two pads of paper, extra socks, extra hat, and binoculars. No wonder I was tuckered out; my backpack probably weighed forty pounds!

I looked at the trail ahead and saw that it snaked through some difficult terrain, complete with ice-covered boulders. If I was going to climb to the summit and still make it down the mountain in daylight, I had to get moving. But what to do about the backpack? I decided to hide it off the trail and go the rest of the way without it.

Maybe it was psychological but I felt stronger without it and I made it to the summit in the next 30 minutes. Below me there was reported to be a good view of the surrounding countryside, but all I could see was a gray landscape that looked something like the ocean on an overcast day. The light snowfall and low cloud cover blocked out most of the vista. Still, the scene was interesting in its own way, especially looking down at the tops of pointed spruce and firs that were white with snow.

The hike down was much easier than going up, and I even remembered to retrieve my backpack. I had been worried about the ice, but found that in the icy spots all I had to do was sit down and I flew down the trail in 15 foot sections on the seat of my nylon-shell pants. In one spot the trail was like a toboggan run, and I careened downward in an exhilarating ride of over 40 feet.

When I got to my car, I took my backpack off and stared at it. Of all the items inside it, the only one I used was the water. Next time, when I'm doing a relatively short climb like today, I'd remove half the items I seldom use. For years I'd been adding stuff to the pack, and today was the first day I noticed my possessions were making my outings more difficult rather than easier. I thought to myself, *how many times in our life do we become beasts of burden to our possessions?*

(The trail to Stowe Pinnacle is east of the center of Stowe, on Upper Hollow Road. A sign for Stowe Pinnacle welcomes you to a small parking area.)

Biking, Hiking and Waterfalls of Greater Stowe
(Stowe, Waterbury, Jeffersonville)

Stowe, Vermont is much more than a ski destination. In the off-season months it offers a variety of activities for the outdoor enthusiast. Here are a few of both the well-known spots and some that are off the beaten path.

South of the village of Stowe is the Waterbury Reservoir and a section of the Mount Mansfield State Forest that are great for both walking and mountain biking. Arriving via Moscow Road at the north end of the reservoir (parking area near the trail sign) there is access to some lower level meadows and to a dirt road that leads up the mountain.

Multiple fields hug the Little River at the base of mounts Ricker and Mansfield. During summer trails are cut in the deep grass to allow easier cycling (using fat tire bikes) and walking along the edges where there aren't any roads. The vistas of the mountains and, when possible, the river, are absolutely worth the trip from town. Stay to the left and follow some of the trails to the water's edge where herons may be hunting in the shallows. The Little River meanders lazily here, its rocky shores inviting wading on hot days. A trail follows the edge of its high embankment closely enough to be of concern at times, but offers beautiful unobstructed views up and down its wide S-turns.

Follow the river southbound toward the reservoir access and loop back through the meadows. At the base of the mountain are some densely-vegetated trails, but most loosely follow the north-south layout below any hills, keeping the trails flat and easy to access.

The road going uphill toward the top of Ricker Mountain is a challenge and you will need to be a strong rider. If you don't mind walking your bike in spots on this uphill road, give it a shot, because the return trip, mostly downhill, is a thrill. For walkers, the uphill climb is quite manageable, and the heavy shade of trees takes the edge off a summer hike. Farther up the hill there are small breaks in the trees, such as an orchard partway up (we're wondering how many bears it attracts in fall). From time to time this road offers a glimpse of the Waterbury Reservoir through the trees, but not much and not for long, just an indication of where you are on the road. If you make it to the top, there's a trail along the ridge toward Ricker Mountain, with difficult mountain bike trails winding their way back down to the parking area – if you still have the legs for them after the tough uphill climb.

The 5.5 mile Stowe Recreation Path must be one of the most-used in the country. Rarely have we seen so many walkers, joggers and cyclists sharing one ribbon of pavement like this on a summer morning. There are many places to jump on and enjoy the path which runs from the village along the West Branch of the Waterbury River up the valley. Be careful crossing Mountain Road if you're staying at one of the local hotels: while the marked pedestrian crossings in the retail district appear to get a lot of respect from motorists, further out of town can be a little dicey. There are several good park-like starting points with parking that we suggest scouting before embarking on a trip to the path.

Paved and fairly blemish-free, the recreation path is a wonder in human conveyance. Patience is a requirement (you're here on vacation, right?) as you are likely to pass and be passed by a multitude of joggers and cyclists along the way. In July look for wild raspberries and blackberries growing along the edges, and stop for a sweet nibble. We used the path to travel into town or just for exercise as it hugs the river, a sedate, soothing presence. Multiple steel truss bridges criss-cross the river, affording a variety of vistas of the water and path. At the far western end horse trails intersect with the paved trail (a stable with trail and buggy rides is here) and in mid-town you find yourself along parking lots for busy restaurant and retail operations, but by and large it's one of the best, most-used paths we've seen. There is even an optional "Quiet Path" designated for joggers and walkers, located off the section of the path near the village.

Just north of Stowe village is impressive Moss Glen Falls, which can be reached by turning off Route 100 onto Randolph Road. It is only a short walk from a small parking area to this beautiful series of falls that drops over 100 feet, making it one of the taller falls in the state. In the spring the water fans out near the base of the falls and in the winter it freezes along the edges into strange looking ice formations. Another trail leads to the top of the falls where you can stare down into the chasm.

Bingham Falls is another series of waterfalls well worth the hike. Although the trail down the hill to the falls is steep, you can reward yourself for the effort by swimming in one of the pools at the base of the falls. Gnarled and ancient hemlock trees shade the falls most of the day, and the water is ice cold. Still, we recommend taking the plunge on a hot summer day. If you don't feel alive after this dip nothing will get you going! Bingham falls is located northwest of Stowe Village off Route 108, just before Smugglers

Notch. During warm weather you will see cars parked in turnoffs on either side of Route 108, and the trial to the falls is on the right side of the road if you are traveling up from the village.

To reach another waterfalls at the Brewster River Gorge (also known as the Jeffersonville Gorge) take the scenic drive through Smugglers Notch where this narrow, rugged road makes several switchback turns passing between steep granite walls (closed in winter). During the War of 1812 smugglers used this road to bring prohibited goods from Canada into the U.S. There are places to pull out along the way, and children will especially enjoy short climbs up the cliffs and exploring nooks, crannies, and small caves.

Brewster River Gorge is located in Jeffersonville, just off Route 108 on Canyon Road, near a covered bridge. There is a large parking area, picnic tables, and a stretch of the river suitable for taking a quick plunge. The trail to the falls follows the river upstream, crossing the river after just a couple hundred feet, and then continues uphill through a hemlock forest. Take a right where the trail forks and you will be at the base of a narrow ravine, where the water cascades around giant boulders. Most of the time the water plunging through this series of small falls can barely be seen, obscured by the rock ledges and truck size boulders. But we still think it's worth the walk because of the dramatic setting, with fewer visitors than Bingham Falls. And like Bingham Falls you can reward yourself with a quick dip in the little pool at the base of the falls.

Located off Sterling Valley Road is Sterling Gorge, with a short trail along the rim of the canyon. Sterling Brook bounces over the boulders and around pines and hemlocks heading south to meet up with the West Branch of the Waterbury River. You can also follow a trail up the hillside along the brook. We did this in the winter on snowshoes and it was a great outing. Another hike we've taken is to Sterling Pond, high up in the hills near Mount Mansfield. This trailhead can be reached off Route 108 where it goes through the notch, at a parking lot for the Long Trail. Nice views await at the end of this moderate hike.

We thought there were even better views at the summit of Mount Hunger, but we had to pay our dues with a hike that some hiking clubs call "advanced." The trailhead is south of Stowe Village on Loomis Hill Road. The 4.4 mile round trip hike passes through forest, across a brook and then up a steep part of the mountain where you will be using hand holds to pick your way around boulders and ledges. When you arrive at the top 360 degree vistas await from the bare rock.

Paddling & Patience on Quiet Waters
(The Green River Reservoir & Area, Hyde Park)

Making the adjustment from our harried lives to the vacation mindset takes effort. It's not always easy to shut off the telephones and block out the everyday noise that spikes our blood pressure, but you will be rewarded, particularly in a quiet setting in Northern Vermont.

If you can carve an afternoon out of your vacation to unplug and let the natural beauty of the area envelop you, we have this suggestion: grab a canoe or kayak and head to Green River Reservoir State Park. It's about 40 minutes north of Stowe in the little town of Hyde Park off a network of dirt roads. It takes patience: give yourself time to unwind, drive with the windows open, leave the technology behind and let the undulations of the country roads seduce you. Or, go because you'll be the only one of your friends who's ever heard of the place. Either way you will be glad you did.

The entrance was unstaffed when we arrived, but at the canoe launch is a kiosk with map of the lake and description of the wildlife in the area. Paper maps may be available here as well, and we suggest taking one with you because a lake looks very different when you're in it, and this one has long fingers extending north and northwest that can be confusing. (Motors are not allowed on the lake, so the people that visit are of a like mind: they are here for the quiet, nature, and a bit of exercise.)

It takes time to paddle up the lake. Note the little numbers nailed to trees. They're remote, paddle-in campsites nestled in the trees and on little islands. Cool, huh? Great idea for next time! And if you enjoy fishing, the lake has smallmouth bass.

You're likely to see a few other paddlers up here on a good day, but there's plenty of room for everyone. We scouted a sunny rock on the far shore, pulled the kayaks up and went for a swim. The water is very clear and quite deep in places (deep enough for us to safely dive off our rock). Another kayaker we saw had brought a little chair and had a grassy island all to herself, the perfect vantage point for enjoying the view of loons diving and resurfacing across the lake.

After a little snooze in the sun, take the kayaks or canoe up the lake's long fingers. Despite some wind, our enjoyable paddle was rewarded with close-ups of many loons, some that objected to our proximity with ruffled feathers, others that rewarded us with their long hooting call. And even better, the kayaks were accompanied briefly by a pair of otters swimming (and sticking their necks up out of the water to check us out!). The shoreline along the north channels is grassy and likely good moose habitat. We will return sometime looking for them.

A few hours here results in a great sense of relaxation and fulfillment. And it continues: the views on the way south toward Stowe are of spectacular meadows and farms stretching to blue mountains in the distance. Your patience and efforts are rewarded.

Lake Willoughby, Mount Pisgah and the WilloughVale Inn
(Westmore and Burke)

Every region of Vermont has its subtle differences, but it's the people of the Kingdom who consider themselves the true Vermonters. Fiercely independent and self-sufficient, they love the Kingdom for what it is – wild, remote and isolated. In a real sense it's a frontier, with frontier hardships. Both the economy (few jobs) and the climate (brutal seven-month winters followed by the quagmire of mud season) seem to conspire against these hill people. Yet they stay and they love it, though I doubt they would use the word "love" to describe their quiet passion for the land. And for some reason, perhaps because it offers independent thinkers the room for individuality, the Kingdom has attracted some of the country's finest writers, such as Edward Hoagland and Howard Frank Mosher.

How did this corner of Vermont get its name? It's said that George Aiken, a former senator from Vermont, was the first to refer to the counties of Orleans, Essex, and Caledonia as the Northeast Kingdom. While fishing in Essex County, he was touched by the beauty surrounding him, and gazing up at the hills said, "This place should have a special name; we should call it the Northeast Kingdom." That was in the 1950s, and since then the Kingdom has shown signs of change, particularly in the number of out-of-state "flatlanders" who have bought summer homes or moved her for good.

One thing I've heard over and over about newcomers is that they come here to escape the suburbs or the city, then the first thing they do is try to change the area to be like their former homes. And what really burns the true Vermonters is seeing a newcomer buy a large block of land and post "No Trespassing" signs, putting prime hunting grounds, used for generations by the locals, off limits. When I consider that scenario, all I can think of is how the Native Americans must have felt when the Europeans told them that not only could they not live in such and such an area, but they couldn't hunt there either.

Mt Pisgah is a great example of the Kingdom's rugged beauty. It looks like half the mountain has been sheared away, as if the glaciers concentrated all their powers here, scouring the land with a grinding force beyond imagination. Thousand-foot-high granite cliffs rise dramatically from the steely waters of Lake Willoughby, disappearing in the dark clouds near the mountain's summit. If the view from below is this incredible I can only imagine what it looks like from the summit.

Normally the climb should take about an hour, but freshets cascade down the trail, making the rocks slick, and I pick my way carefully along the trail. It's May 4, and I'm ahead of black-fly season and apparently ahead of spring as well. A few patches of snow cling stubbornly to low-lying depressions and the wind still has winter's bite. The trees are bare, and the forest looks like a black-and-white picture, highlighted here and there with brown hues.

The trail switches back, then begins a more gradual ascent along the spine of the mountain. Soon I'm at Pulpit Rock, a granite outcrop that juts toward the lake with a sheer drop of about 500 feet. I sit at the edge of the cliff and marvel at the scene. Willoughby stretches out below, long and narrow, locked in on the east by Mount Pisgah and on the west by Mount Hor. It's said that the lake reminds people of the fjords of Norway and from this vantage point that's exactly what I thought. With clouds partially shrouding the surrounding mountains, and the lake a slate gray, the whole scene was a haunting one, giving me the feeling of aloneness. Nothing stirred on the mountain, and nothing stirred below; all living things were still in their dens, nests, burrows, or homes.

Open heights have always made me uncomfortable, and this one is no exception, giving me a touch of vertigo. So instead of standing, I slide off the rock on my backside, so as not to risk rising suddenly and becoming dizzy. Why is it, I wonder, that I enjoy riding in airplanes (even going up in a glider once), when exposed ledges like this get under my skin?

Still more climbing ahead. Sprinkles of raindrops patter on dry leaves and a western breeze rocks the treetops. The silence is broken by the cry of a raven, circling alone just above the trees. At least something else is alive up here, but ravens, like turkey vultures, remind me of Poe's dark lines rather than the glories of nature.

I'm sweating heavily now, despite an air temperature in the thirties. Another half hour of climbing brings me to a grove of white birch mixed with spruce and fir, and I rest on a log, taking a long pull of water from my bottle. Crushing a sprig of spruce in my hand, I breathe deeply of the pungent evergreen, gathering strength from the scent, savoring the smell of the North Country.

Back on my feet the trail gets narrower, pulling away from the lake. More snow in the gullies, more softwoods. I've read that arctic plants, such as sweet broom and mountain saxifrage, grow on the cliffs, and I believe it – the temperature seems to drop every five minutes. I look at my watch – 3:30. Just enough time for a dash to the summit and then down before dark. But there's five inches of snow on the trail now, and mine are the only footsteps. I pass an exposed area of bedrock with a view of Burke Mountain, but it's not the northern panorama I'm after.

I know I'm close to summit, know I'm just minutes away from one of Vermont's best views, but I can't find the trail. There is heavy, icy snow everywhere, some pockets rising to my knees. I *think* I know which direction the Upper Overlook is, but what if I'm wrong? I pause, debating my options. If I get lost or twist an ankle, no one knows I'm here. Ten or twenty years ago I might have pushed on a bit farther, probably achieved my goal, and probably would have been perfectly safe. But probably is no guarantee, so I wait some more and think.

Taking time to assess a situation *before* you plod ahead is wisdom. For me, that wisdom comes from spending so much time in the woods (which brings respect), age (I've crossed the 50 mark), and a couple of close calls in the past (a mishap on a Vermont river and a brief period of being lost in northern Maine). There is really no decision to make. Only a fool would take a risk here. I'm tired, it's approaching dusk, and the temperatures are at levels where hypothermia could kill me before the night's over. Making the wrong decision, because of the siren call of the summit, is what gets some peak-baggers killed.

My backpack has a few emergency supplies, such as matches, water, compass, whistle, and multi-purpose knife, but a little bad luck – like swirling snow or pouring rain – could make a night in the woods a recipe for disaster. If I ever get into climbing in a big way, maybe I'll buy one of those space-age thermal emergency blankets that is a proven lifesaver. But the most important survival tool is the thing between your ears, particularly when you use it to ask yourself, "What is the safe course of action?" For me, just an intermediate-level climber, turning around is the right thing to do.

I start back down the trail, thinking how ridiculous it is that I was so focused on reaching the top; I overlooked enjoying the journey up. There should be no goal, just enjoyment of the outing. If you reach the top, great. If you can climb all the really big mountains, the 4,000-footers, that's great too, if you enjoy the process, the journey, the thrill of discovery. But if you try to "collect" a mountain, notch it in your belt; you miss the very essence of the experience. Mountains bring a spiritual renewal, and the physical act of climbing is the therapy, the cleansing of the soul for the summit. But the *whole* mountain is a sacred place, not just the summit, as I find out on the way down. Exhausted, cold and disappointed, the mountain gives me a wake-up call in the form of a crimson flash. It's the red crest of a pileated woodpecker, swooping through the trees, ringing out its odd call. In the gray forest, still under the grip of winter, the reward of the woodpecker brought a smile to me. This is why I do it, I thought, the little elemental things that go unnoticed when you're inside, surrounded by artificial light and sound. And I'm here for the physical joy of climbing, no different than the "high" runners get.

Every sport has its highs, but mountain-climbing thrills have to be tempered with logic, especially climbs in the cold-weather months. Every year someone overestimates his strength, and underestimates the weather, winding up in real trouble on a forlorn peak. Survivors often tell a similar story, how a front moved in so quickly they found themselves in a near-whiteout when just an hour before there had been unlimited sunshine. Temperatures can plunge twenty degrees, conspiring with the wind to sap strength. The mountain and the rock are indifferent to pleas for help.

Once at the bottom I drive south looking for something, anything, hot, to eat or drink. In East Burke I hit the brakes. The little town crossroads has a café, ice cream stand, pub, market, country store, and sports shop. I fill up on hot coffee, as much food as I consume, and poke around the country store. I'm warmed up in no time, and thankful to be in civilization, but not in a shopping mall, which I avoid like the plague.

More comforts follow when I check into the WilloughVale Inn, on the northern end of Lake Willoughby, where I immediately soak in a hot bath. Is there a better feeling after a day outdoors in the cold?

The WilloughVale Inn, with its fine restaurant, is a magnet for both locals and travelers, where both can come together and trade stories over the cherry wood bar in the pub. During dinner I talked with an elderly gentleman named John who lives on the lake. All of us have a special place, and he describes his in a poignant way:

"I'm seventy-five now, but I remember the first time I came here on vacation when I was ten years old – I had the feeling I was home. Even when I lived in different areas of the U.S., I still considered Willoughby my home. It took me until I was almost sixty to finally settle here for good, but now I wake up and look right down the gap, all the way to Burke Mountain, just like I dreamed."

I know exactly what he meant. I had the same feeling the first time I stayed at the old Rutledge Inn on Lake Morey in Vermont, and have dreamed of living on that lake ever since. Vermont has a way of getting in your blood, of tugging at you until you come back. I went to college in Vermont, then bought my cabin at the edge of the Kingdom shortly after. My brother Mark loved the state so much he moved here for good a few years back, and someday maybe I'll do the same.

The best inns usually have a top-notch library of regional books, and the WilloughVale is no exception. The books on Lake Willoughby keep me up much later than I intend, but when you read about other's experiences in the very place you are exploring, who can think of sleep? I read that the origin of the name Mount Pisgah is biblical – a mountain in Jordan from which Moses saw the Promised Land – and Mount Hor was named for the place where Moses' brother Aaron died and was buried. Another book says that Abraham climbed Pisgah, but was stopped fifty feet from the summit! Maybe it was the curse of Abraham that forced me off the mountain.

The lake, I learn, is almost five miles long, less than a mile wide, and said to be 308 feet deep. Such depths make it a first-class cold-water fishery, with landlocked salmon, some monster browns, and lake trout that usually take the state's annual record. In fact, Vermont's current record lake trout, a thirty-four pounder, was pulled from Willoughby. And like all deep lakes, this one has its monster sightings. In 1986 a woman from New Jersey saw a large aquatic creature, and fifteen years earlier a two-humped creature was sighted. Even as far back as 1868 *The Caledonian* reported that a boy killed a great snake in the lake: "Rushing boldly upon the monster he severed the body with a sickle. The two pieces were found to be 23 feet."

Surprisingly, instead of draining south like most New England waterways, the lake drains north into Lake Memphremagog, then continues to Canada and the St. Lawrence. In the mid nineteenth century, Willoughby was a popular resort referred to as the "Lucerne of America." The Lake House at the southern end and Gilman's Tavern at Westmore Village housed guests from across the country, while steamboats carried them on tours. The lake inspired visitors in the twentieth century as well, as evidenced in a poem written in 1911 by Eva Margaret Smith, simply called *Lake Willoughby*:

> *Watched over by a vast sentinels of rock*
> *Surrounded by the gloom of forests deep*

Thy waves leap high in boisterous playfulness
Or peaceful calm in sleep.
The sunset glory falls on Pisgah's height,
Clothing that rugged form with beauty rare,
While numerous waves lap gently on the shore,
A lullaby to care.
O beauteous lake and forest-laden hills
Where shadow fall and endless breezes blow
Almost though seemest in our troubled age
An Eden here below.

WilloughVale Inn:
www.willoughvale.com
802-525-4123

Mount Pigsah area

Mount Pigsah (USGS 7.5' Sutton Provisional) and Mount Hor (USGS 7.5' Sutton) are both located in Willoughby State Forest, spanning 7,300 acres. The trail head for Mount Pigsah can be found about half a mile south of Lake Willoughby at a parking lot on Route 5A (the Mount Hor parking area is about 1.8 miles up a dirt road that leads west from the Mount Pigsah parking area.)

Victory Bog, Stone Houses, Porcupines and Trout
(North Concord, Granby, Victory, Brownington, Barton to the Lamoille River)

At dawn I drive to Victory Bog. It's a unique natural area, covering roughly 20,000 acres in a valley which has the second largest tract of boreal forest in Vermont. Within this basin are 1,800 acres of wetlands between the villages of North Concord and the Gallup Mills section of Granby. Curling through the valley is the Moose River and Bog Brook.

Wildlife abounds – moose, bear, coyote, beaver, fox, mink fisher, otter, muskrat, bobcat – if it lives in Vermont, chances are it lives here. But the real draw for a nature lover is the abundant bird life in the diverse habitat of marsh, bog, spruce forest, red maple swamps and rivers carving through hardwoods. Great blue heron, bitterns, and green heron stalk the marsh, while osprey and kingfishers perch on dead tree limbs scanning the water for fish. Red-tailed hawks circle above, and marsh hawks hover over meadows looking for mice and voles. Smaller birds such as swamp swallows, spotted sandpipers, and redwing blackbirds are commonly seen, along with a wide variety of ducks. Great horned owls make nocturnal forays into the marsh, looking to swoop down on rabbits and skunks. And more than one motorist, driving through the fog-filled bog at night, has caught the long shape of what appeared to be a mountain lion in his headlights.

The plant life is as diverse as the wildlife. Indian cucumber, leatherleaf, sheep laurel and countless other plants, including the carnivorous sundew and pitcher plant, thrive deep in the interior in a twenty-five acre shrub boreal bog. Tamarack and spruce climb up the hills, while alders and meadowsweet crowd along the channel of the Moose River.

From North Concord a forlorn stretch of gravel road runs through the heart of the Victory Bog, following the Moose River upstream, past the "frontier town" of Victory and into the Victory Bog Wildlife Management Area. Victory has a population of 62 people, but at one time it had seven villages, six sawmills, three post offices, a hotel, five schools, and its own railroad spur with four stations. In a thousand years I would have never guessed that such a thriving community was tucked away up these hills.

The road through Victory Bog passes through dark forests that give way to wetlands where a grassy marsh stretches far in all directions until encircled by rising mountains. Set up on a raised bed of gravel, the road allows one

to cruise through marsh that normally would be seen only from a canoe.

Two young moose are lying down in a sedge meadow, and rise to their feet as my car inches closer. I kill the engine and roll down the window. They rise, turn their backs on me, and trot off, their hooves making a sucking sound in the muck.

Now I'm outside of the car, and the silence hits me. But it's not the desolate, lonely silence I felt a couple days earlier on Mount Pigsah, but rather the silence of a sleeping beast. There are signs of spring in the greenery, and ducks are winging their way back and forth over the marsh. The scent of dank, rich earth fills the air. It feels as though the marsh is ready to explode from its winter slumber, a life force ready to spring from the primordial ooze.

I try to walk along the river, but the ground is too soft and the trees and shrub too tangled to get far. Instead, not far from the road, I find little pockets of dry land from which to fish near the water's edge. I only fish for a short time, then go back to the car, where I look over the atlas, noting that there are barely any roads east of Victory Bog, all the way to the Connecticut River.

It's 9 a.m. now, and I think of a big breakfast in Lyndonville. A car comes by and the driver asks if I'm lost. I tell him I'm just exploring, looking for wildlife.

"Well," he says, "about a quarter mile down the road I just saw a big bull moose; it's probably still there."

That's all I need to hear. Breakfast is forgotten. I shoulder my pack, attach the zoom lens to my camera, and follow the road deeper into Victory Bog.

After photographing the moose and enjoying a big breakfast, I turn my attention to the countless number of gravel roads to explore in the countryside to the northwest of Lake Willoughby, passing through Brownington and Barton. Brownington is known to history lovers because of the Old Stone House Museum, which bills itself as "the rarest kind of museum: a building as fascinating as the collection it houses." Made of granite blocks, and looking like a fortress, it was designed and erected in the 1830s by a man believed to be America's first black college graduate and first black legislator, the Reverend Alexander Twilight. Twilight was on a mission: he quarried the stone, dressed the blocks, and dragged them to the site with a single ox, where he spent three years of his life constructing his stone house. Although the 30-room monument looks like a garrison, Twilight used it as a school where he taught the region's children.

The Twilight story is one of courage and individuality, and I especially like it because it's so different than the Irasburg Affair of 1968, where racial prejudice forced a black family to leave the little town of Irasburg. It's a sad story, and was used as the inspiration for Howard Frank Mosher's dark novel, *A Stranger in the Kingdom*. Every region has its good people and bad, and the Kingdom is no exception.

Near The Old Stone House is Prospect Hill, just up the road a bit, next to a tiny church in Brownington. I walk to the top of the hill and to the observation platform, and drink in the scene. Two layers of cloud cover are floating over the valley, one far overhead blocking out the sun, and another narrow band at treetop level. Between these stratums, mile after endless mile of mountains stretch to the horizons. The distinctive gap of Willoughby, framed by the twin mountains of Pisgah and Hor, dominates the southern horizon, while in the foreground the steeple of a church knifes through the low cloud cover.

I meditate on the platform, thankful to be alive in such a place of beauty. Then, as I'm leaving, I notice a dark outline in a huge old sugar maple at the corner of the field. On closer inspection I see that it's a porcupine, nipping off the buds of the tree. I should be content to take my picture and leave, but instead I climb the tree, first up the trunk then inching out on the branch, hoping for the perfect photograph. But wildlife never cooperates. I figure the porcupine will climb farther out on the branch, but instead it makes a U-turn and begins its descent – with me directly in its path. For a brief moment I'm face-to-face with this beady-eyed creature, separated by about five feet, with the gap narrowing as it keeps coming.

Porcupines can't throw their quills, but this one won't need to in another second, and I almost fall out of the maple, sliding backwards, scraping my hands, doing an awkward shimmy back down. Serves me right.

Porcupines hold a fascination for me, probably dating back to my boyhood when two of them scared the life out of me. My family was staying at a remote cabin in the Berkshires, and my brother and I slept on the porch. Sometime in the middle of one night, blood-curdling screams and screeches – no more than a few feet away – woke us in terror. The screams were high-pitched and maniacal. When they subsided, we mustered the courage to venture outside with our flashlights, scanning the ground. We could see nothing and turned to go back in the porch when a shrill cry pierced our ears, coming not from the woods but from directly overhead in an old apple tree. With shaking hands, we shone our flashlights on the culprits – two porcupines. Maybe they were fighting, or maybe they were making love, but whatever it was we both never forgot those screams. Only the wailing bark of a fox floating through a dark night is as scary.

Porcupines will den anywhere it is dry, favoring granite ledges, but also using old culverts and even outhouses! (I had one appear in my outhouse, and yes, there was a close call of the posterior kind.) It's a lackadaisical animal, feeling secure in all its 30,000 quills, and it usually moves slowly. But when threatened it can whip its tail around with surprising speed, and more than one dog has gotten a nose full of quills. When a porcupine quill enters the body it absorbs moisture and expands, working deeper, even as much as an inch a day. If it hits a vital organ, it's lights out. But in spite of its armor, there are a few predators, like the mountain lion and fisher, who can kill porcupines. The fisher does so by circling the porcupine, nipping at it exposed face and tiring it through a long dance of blood loss and death.

After the porcupine incident I ramble over to the village of Orleans in Barton to watch the rainbows run the Willoughby River. Each spring the fish leave Lake Memphremagog to spawn in the Willoughby. There is a small waterfall here, and after waiting and watching for twenty minutes I see a five-pounder leap the falls in a silver blur. Anglers line the banks below the falls, primarily fishing with spawn sacks and bait in hopes of dueling with these Memphremagog rainbows. My rod is in the car, but with dozens of anglers already scattered along the river it doesn't look like my cup of tea.

The best part of trout fishing for me is the "hunting" aspect, walking carefully up the river, searching out productive pockets and trying for the perfect presentation. It calls for stealth and full attention, whereby you become absorbed in the pursuit, and time seems suspended. Hours can go by or just minutes, but either way you forget about every other aspect of your life – and that's the beauty of it. If I'm in one spot for long, whether it's in a boat or on shore, the thrill just isn't there.

So I head southwestward to the Lamoille River, an old favorite. It's a good-sized river, rising in the Kingdom in the village of Greensboro and flowing westward, out of the Kingdom, covering 85 miles before reaching Lake Champlain. Its headwaters hold brook trout and rainbows, with good growth rates due to dissolved minerals, such as magnesium and calcium that naturally leach into the water from the soil and rocks. Over the years I've fished the river probably close to a hundred times, with good success on most occasions. And it will take another hundred times to explore sections of the river I've yet to walk.

Just about the entire run of the Lamoille holds trout. The stretch along Route 16, where the river runs shallow and swift, has small trout in the riffles and pools. Even in Hardwick center, trout hold behind rocks in the rapids near the Village Restaurant, and farther west in Wolcott, where train whistles crack the silence as they rumble through the covered railroad bridge, trout hide beneath undercut banks. In Morrisville and Johnson the river broadens, and holes up to 30 feet deep hold brown trout of legendary proportions. Between Jeffersonville and Fairfax trout somehow survive in the relatively warm water, mixed with bass and other warm-water species. Even the mouth of the Lamoille gave me the gift of good fishing, not of trout, but of a northern pike, three feet long, battling for more than half an hour.

The tributaries are productive as well – the Wild Branch, Green River, Gihon River, North Branch and the Brewster River. Just saying their names brings back memories of the people I fished with and even the trout themselves. Fish may not have a personality, but given enough time to reflect on a memorable day of fishing, I usually think of a particular fish caught or lost on that outing. And over time the trout becomes not just a fish, but an individual creature blending in with the whole experience. The friend I fish with, the river, and the trout become an important memory, and memories are really as much of who we are as any other facet of the mind.

Unknown Pond, Lost Nation, and Indian Raids
(Northeast Kingdom, Island Pond Area)

I was lost on the back roads in northeast Vermont. Facing the proverbial "you can't get there from here," I sat on a bench in Newport and studied my atlas to see how to reach New Hampshire.

The map revealed there was no road heading directly eastward along the border and into New Hampshire. In fact there weren't many roads at all in this uppermost section of the Northeast Kingdom. It looked like the town of Holland and Norton, directly east of Derby Line, consisted of a huge expanse of forest. The locals called the woods The Hurricane, but the two I asked could not remember how it got its name. Since there was no passable road connecting Holland to Norton, it appeared the best route would be to head southeast toward Morgan on Route 111, passing Seymour Lake, and then continue on into Island Pond. There, I could pick up Route 114 and head northeast toward the border and then follow it all the way to New Hampshire.

An hour passed as I studied the atlas, intrigued by the some of the names it showed. There was Lost Nation, an apparent crossroads just south of Island Pond. And even the name Island Pond was somewhat unusual for a village, named after the pond adjacent to the town. The term pond didn't seem to be the right one either, because this "pond" was over a mile long spanning 600 acres and deep enough to support trout. When I think of a pond the image I conjure is a small, shallow body of water where pickerel and bass live. In fact most ponds that meet my definition usually don't even have cottages or homes on them, with Vermonters preferring the deep, spring-fed lakes. Directly north of Island Pond, however, there was such a pond, and it had a great name to boot: Unknown Pond. It was situated deep in the woods in the township of Averys Gore. As I studied the atlas, and considered trying to explore this town, I realized Averys Gore probably had no more than five or six people living in it. There was no village center, nor did there appear to be a paved road, or any road for that matter that went from one end of the town to the other. Next to Avery's Gore was Warren Gore, and next to that was Warners Grant, which also had no roads going through it.

Seeing the term gore and grant got me thinking I was in a strange place indeed, surmising that a gore was a wooded valley and a grant was a territory that never quite became a town. I also began to realize that part of my route would be the same one the Indians of St. Francis (on the St. Lawrence River in Quebec) used when raiding the colonies. They would travel from Quebec to the Connecticut River by first paddling the St. Francis and Magog Rivers into Memphremagog, then continue southeast up the Clyde River into Island Pond, and then overland through forest, probably following the Nulhegan River as the quickest route the Connecticut River. Once on the Connecticut they could either canoe with the current southward or in the winter use snowshoes and walk right down the frozen river.

In the late 1600's and early 1700's the settlements in Massachusetts on the Connecticut River where the northern most outposts and towns like Deerfield were hit repeatedly. Later as settlement pushed up the river, the natives attacked the Charlestown New Hampshire where The Fort at No. 4 was located. And who could blame the Indians. Many of these natives that settled at St. Francis were actually from villages in Massachusetts and Maine which were wiped out during the battles of King Philip's War. If you look at these raids from the Indian perspective they were merely striking a blow against the people that took their homelands.

I headed southeast on a back road, seeing exactly one other car in a 20-mile stretch. I found my way onto Route 111 heading southeast and then onto Route 114 going northeast eventually paralleling the Canadian border. The drive had many stops with one brief black bear sighting and several stops at different streams to fish for small brook trout. I never did make it to Unknown Pond, so it will stay unknown to me, but the ride was through some remote country, and it made me want to come back with a bicycle. I wouldn't have to worry about traffic.

Moose, Otter and Raiders
(Northeast Kingdom, Seymour Lake Area)

I set out early one morning to explore the network of dirt roads in quest of a secluded stream to try my luck for native brook trout. I managed to catch a couple but the best part of the day was the unexpected events. On one river, I was wading in the water when I heard a splash, and turned my head in time to see an otter surface about twenty feet away. The otter had apparently just slid down the slide it had made on the riverbank. The slide looked like a mini toboggan-run in the mud. I continued fishing and five minutes later I saw another otter or perhaps the same one, shoot down the slide as if to make sure I saw how much fun it was. Who knows, if the water was a little warmer I might have given it a try.

The first moose I saw was a youngster, feeding on aquatic plants by the side of the road on Route 111 in Morgan, Vermont, just a few miles below the border with Canada. Usually when I see wildlife, I either don't have my camera or there is not enough light for a decent photo. But on this day my camera was lying on the passenger seat and the setting sun was shining directly on the moose, illuminating it and the marsh in a golden light. I was about 50 feet from the moose and decided not to risk scaring it away by opening the car door and instead rolled down the window and got my shots from inside the car. The moose lifted its head, water streaming from its mouthful of plants, and I clicked away with the camera. Later I saw a moose that dwarfed the one I'd seen that morning. This one was a full-grown bull with a huge rack of antlers. It was lapping up the water in a muddy spot by the side of the road, probably because it was laced with salt that was spread on the road during the winter. I eased out of my car and walked to an opening in the trees where I could photograph the moose. Just as I raised my camera, the moose lifted its head, took a step to toward me, glaring. If this had occurred during the fall rut, I probably would have climbed the nearest tree, but because it was summer I was hoping the bull moose might tolerate my presence. I froze while the moose considered whether I was a threat or not, and luckily it must have decided I was harmless, and it resumed its drinking. That's when I exhaled with relief, calmed my shaky hands and managed to get several photos. The best photo, however, still can't compare with the moment when our eyes were locked, one species to another, communicating with a look, and the moose had clearly said "that's close enough."

This area wasn't always so quiet, nor did all confrontations like mine with the moose end peaceably. During the French and Indian Wars, Major Robert Rogers led a group of his Rangers on a daring mission to attack the Indians at the Village of Saint Francis, Canada in 1759. The raid was successful, but the Rangers equally daunting task of returning to the safety of the Colonies was in question. As soon as the village had been burned, Rogers immediately led his men south, past Lake Memphremagog into Vermont's Northeast Kingdom. Several hundred Natives and French were on his heels with revenge on their minds.

Rogers split his men into smaller groups to make them harder to track while also hoping they would have a better chance to hunt game, because they had been without food for a number of days. One party south, passing by Lake Seymour, and another party was a few miles away passing by Norton Pond. The Norton Pond party, led by Lieutenant Dunbar, met a tragic fate at the pond's southern shore. The Indians caught up with them here, and after a brief fight, all but three of Dunbar's 20 men were killed, their bodies washing downstream into the Pherrins River.

And so I visited the Pherrins, trudging around its soft banks and through the woods, hoping to find a stone marker where the men were attacked. I searched but apparently this bit of history has been all but forgotten because there were only alders and spruce, but no marker. Back at the car I read more about the attack to see what happened next, and hopefully follow another trail of Rangers. But the next few lines in my history the book made me pause. A second group of starving Rangers, led by Lieutenant Campbell, followed this same path three days later and came upon the mangled bodies of Dunbar's men. I'll let Campbell tell you what happened next. "I lost control of my men as they fell like wolves upon ye horribly cut up remains (of the dead men) and proceeded to cut off strips of flesh and bolt them raw."

Yikes. Who would have thought this peaceful corner of Vermont would have been the scene of cannibalism? And so I took up the trail of Campbell's party, who were saved from certain starvation by consuming the flesh of their own comrades. Down the Pherrins River they went, into Island Pond, then eastward along the Nulhegan River and ultimately to the Connecticut River where they were rescued.

I couldn't help think about the contrast between my relaxing day and the ones the Rangers had here 250 years ago. I used to say I wish I was born 300 years ago, now I'm not so sure.

Bikes and Blooms at the Wildflower Inn in the Northeast Kingdom
(Lyndonville and East Burke)

Upon entering our suite at the Wildflower Inn on Darling Hill Road in Lyndonville our eyes were immediately drawn to the landscape outside the windows: vibrant green hills dotted with cows and cut by fences, tall stands of spruce accenting the quilt. Beyond the immediate slopes were darker green swaths of trees, and beyond those, the blue humps of Vermont's mountains.

Then, something moved toward us: a person on a bicycle, coming up through a field along the fence line. Dressed in bright colors, she pedaled hard to approach the farm's silo and level ground like a bird alighting with a flutter of wings. At that moment, we were torn: stroll the grounds of the Inn and enjoy the gardens and vistas, or join those on the adjacent Kingdom Trails network for an afternoon of mountain biking? Thanks to the proximity of the inn, we were able to get our fill of both in 24 hours.

The Wildflower Inn has been a 30-year-old labor of love for Jim and Mary O'Reilly. Back then the young couple was readying to move out of the country to pursue Jim's engineering career. The farm was for sale and he found himself outnumbered by Mary and her family who pushed him to purchase it. "They lobbied hard for it," he remembers. "Then we bought it and it was like, 'now we own a dairy farm, what do we do with it?'"

What they did was hold onto most of the farmland and convert the buildings to accommodate adventure seekers and families. The O'Reillys raised eight children here, some of whom still work at the inn, while trying to stay atop the ever-changing tourist trade. Jim O'Reilly says they retain most of the original 500 acres of farmland purchased in 1984, but abandoned the idea of hiring a manager to run the place. It was opened as an inn in 1985 with four guest rooms in the main house.

By 1990 many outbuildings were eliminated and the vision of the inn with sumptuous grounds was taking shape with much exertion: with the help and involvement of Mary's parents, the couple built many of the lush gardens and put in place things like a children's activity center and petting zoo in old barn buildings. The result is a year-round destination for a wide variety of travelers.

Its 24 rooms and suites occupy both sides of a quiet dirt road with million-dollar views and plenty of serene garden spaces to enjoy. We couldn't decide between the Heaven's Bench knob overlooking the farm or the gazebo in a quiet field behind the buildings as our favorite place to enjoy the vistas. There were flowers in bloom along walls and walkways everywhere we strolled on the property, and we enjoyed watching three massive golden-haired Belgian draft horses trot up from their pasture to the barn at feeding time.

The O'Reilly's conversion of the property coincided with a push for the area to expand its tourist trade from winter-only skiers to year-round with the formation of the Kingdom Trails Association, a cooperative effort of more than 50 landowners to create a network of over 100 miles of mountain biking trails centered in nearby East Burke.

For a fraction of the cost of a ski lift ticket, mountain bikers can get a day pass and a map to enjoy the trails, choosing among easy, moderate and black diamond-difficulty ratings. The majority fall in the "blue" or moderately challenging category.

The Kingdom Trails network allows several local inns to claim "bike from your door" convenience for the trails as they form a web covering the hillsides and ravines from Burke Mountain to Lyndonville. Likewise, inns such as the Wildflower offer special amenities for cyclists, including a locked storage room, a designated area to clean bikes, supervised children's activities so parents may take off for a few hours, a great menu of restorative food for after cycling and the option of a shower and changing room to use after check-out.

Our first ride took us from the Wildflower to Heaven's Bench, a knob overlooking the property. Since several of the outlets for Heaven's Bench are black diamond trails, we enjoyed the views but turned to take the Bill Magill and Sugarhouse Run routes northward to East Darling Hill Road instead. These took us through fields and woods of fragrant evergreens.

One of our favorite parts of the ride was pedaling through micro-climates. In the woods the air felt cool, moist and scented with ferns. Then as we emerged into open fields the warmth of the sun embraced us, and we'd take our eyes off the trail and drink in the dazzling vistas of blue-green mountains in the distance and colorful fields of green grass and yellow black-eyed susans at the wood's edge. The trails we rode on were in remarkably good shape considering it had rained hard just two days before. They are comprised of relatively smooth hard-packed dirt with very few tree roots or rocks to trip you up.

Once at The Inn at Mountain View Farm we chose the green (easiest) Loop trail around the back of the property, enjoying different angles of the farm's giant restored barns. Then we got on Beamis, the trail that took us along the edges of farm fields back to the Wildflower, startling a "rafter" of turkeys ahead of us on the trail (we had to look that term up).

Between Beamis and the West Branch of the Passumpsic River are lots of more challenging trails that wind through trees and run down steep dirt paths. Troll Stroll and Tap and Die are two challenging trails there that include lots of switchbacks and weave tightly among the trees. The beauty of Kingdom Trails' variety is that the multitude of trails allows novices and advanced riders to stay somewhat together during a day's ride, often on nearly parallel trails, with options to meet at the far end. On weekends there is even a snack bar set up under tall pines near where the Fox Run and Violet's Outback trails intersect and it's heavily used by large groups as a meeting place.

Along with the variety of trails are opportunities to learn new biking skills. Because the trail system is so spread out, I often find myself alone on a section and therefore able to attempt a difficult black diamond trail, like steeply banked turns or narrow bridges, with the option of walking the bike out if it gets too tough. And saving face in the process.

While the trails stretch for more than a mile on both sides of Darling Hill Road, the epicenter of the action is in East Burke, where the Kingdom Trails office sells passes and riders by the dozen gather in the big grass parking lot nearby. Along the main street there are a gas station (which sold me a life-saving package of allergy pills one day), an ice cream stand, a friendly (and very busy) bike store that offers rentals, an apres-bike restaurant and a general store with great sandwiches. All are great opportunities to talk to other riders and learn about gear, the best trails that weekend and events like festivals.

Another mile to the east of East Burke is the Burke Mountain ski area, which makes use of the ski lifts in the offseason by carrying riders up to the top of expert-only trails. According to Jim O'Reilly, snow-less winters will soon see more bikers – fat tire riders – rather than no business at all.

Even the most experienced, most energetic rider can't expect to cover all of Kingdom Trails in a weekend. Along with the many miles of trails are some serious hill climbs (I'll admit to pushing my bike up part of Pinkham Road to reach Magill Fields trails). The best strategy I've found is to carry a snack and lots of water, and plan for a restorative lunch, perhaps with a dip in the Passumpsic to soothe tired legs.

True to mountain biking roots, the parking lot behind the Kingdom Trails ticket office in East Burke becomes something of a bike festival on weekends. Riders meet there, take breaks, work on their bikes and nap in the shade of their cars. Tool and information sharing is commonplace, as are group picnics. It's a great new twist on the old Vermont tradition of neighbors helping one another.

Wildflower Inn:
www.wildflowerinn.com
802-626-8310

Lake Memphremagog and Water's Edge B&B
(Newport)

We pulled up at the Water's Edge B&B on a warm summer afternoon, Lake Memphremagog stretching almost from its front door to the Canadian border five miles to the north. There were people sitting on the dock, contemplating the silvery expanse of water. One got up and approached us. "I need to warn you," he said, "not to sit on that dock on the day you're supposed to check out and go home. You will never want to leave."

A day later, we completely understood the man's humorous warning. We'd biked to the international border along Lake Road that passed by expansive farm fields and views of the lake, used our paddleboards to explore the lakefront, visited downtown Newport for dinner and crossed the ridge toward the town of Newport Center where the sunset over distant blue mountains was spectacular.

Memphremagog, called Magog by the locals is huge: a 25-mile-long lake, with three miles in Vermont and its remaining 22 miles waters in Quebec. It's a two-tier fishery with trout and salmon holding to the deeper water in the summer and warm water species such as smallmouth bass and walleye closer to the surface. Its major tributaries, the Clyde, Barton River, and Black River are all in Vermont and they all flow north, unlike most other rivers in New England. (Northern Star sightseeing boats, offer a variety of day and sunset cruises on the Lake from its home port of Newport.)

The Water's Edge, run for more than 20 years by Patricia Bryan, is a well appointed home of big guest rooms and modern amenities. While she's quiet and unassuming, the owner has traveled the world herself, drawn as she says to the water everywhere she goes. In the B&B's huge open living/dining area Pat told us about bears in her apple trees during summer and the villages of fishermen and their families that spring up on the ice when the giant lake freezes.

Peace enveloped us in the evening, tucked away in our guestroom with windows open to catch the lake's nighttime air. In the morning, strong coffee and a hearty omelets breakfast with biscuits and a creamy honey spread got us off to a good start. While the accommodations are beautiful, well kept and most relaxing, we can only recommend this location to dog lovers as the owner keeps several large, friendly dogs of her own. The other guests we met brought their own pooch and enjoyed an enviable suite of big rooms with an attached second-floor deck overlooking the lake.

There are just two other options for bed and breakfasts in the area. We liked the looks of Cliff Haven, just up Lake Road toward the Canadian border, and considered the in-town convenience of Little Gnesta close to the action in Newport. We were told the town will likely look different next time we wander through, as the Jay Peak ski area owner plans to site a hotel with retail space right downtown.

Despite its proximity to the Canadian border, Newport is easily accessible by Interstate 91, making a visit in any season easy and worthwhile. We launched our paddleboards just north of the B&B, at the Whipple Point boat ramp off Strawberry Acres Road and plied the relatively shallow waterfront north and south. Thanks to the size of the lake, the speedboats that passed barely caused a ripple. And we had the opportunity to wave to passengers on one of Newport's attractions, the Northern Star ferry that offers several cruises a day, with meals, for a reasonable price.

An interesting aspect of Newport and Vermont in general is the way local businesses support one another. When choosing a place to dine in town, we found the Northeast Kingdom Tasting Center, a former department store space turned into a gallery of local goods by several food-related businesses. All offered tastes of their products from spirits to cheeses to maple candy, making for a gastronomic kaleidoscope.

Water's Edge B&B:
www.watersedge-bed-and-breakfast.com
802-334-1840

Northern Star Lake Cruises:
www.vermontlakecruises.com
802-487-0234

The U.S. and Canada, Cheek to Cheek
(Derby)

On a cool spring day I visited Derby Line on the Canadian border. Rather than take the well traveled Route 5 northeastward, I found some obscure roads along Memphremagog's eastern shore then cut into Derby Line on Beebe Road and Elm Street. Sometimes you learn more about a town by viewing its side streets first. There were rolling fields and modest but handsome homes leading toward a large ballfield and park by the town's center.

When I hit Route 5, the customs station was just ahead. I did not want to go through customs because my car was a mess, almost every available interior inch packed with my traveling necessities from fishing waders to cameras. With my luck I'd be the random check, and they spend hours hauling out the mess, looking at the trout in my cooler and wondering what nationality it was. So I parked my car and walked to the customs station where I asked directions to the Haskell Library. The officer pointed the way and within two minutes I stood in front of this fascinating library where the border of the two countries cuts diagonally through the building. The exterior walls were also rather odd, with the first floor made of huge granite blocks and the second floor from yellow bricks.

The library was open and I stopped inside and was delighted to see that in the sunny sitting room with stained glass windows there was line painted on the floor showing exactly where the border was. I found a history book about Derby (Derby Line is a village within the town) and pulled a chair up over the line, hoping for inspiration having one cheek in Canada and the other in the U.S. I read that before Derby became a town, the states of Vermont, Massachusetts, New Hampshire and New York all laid claim to the territory. I also learned that among the earliest settlers were two Abenaki Indians, called Joe and Molly, who had an interesting life, even meeting General George Washington during the Revolution. Besides residing in Derby, the couple lived not far from my cabin at a lake in Cabot and Danville. Because Joe and Molly warned the local residents of a possible Indian attack, they named the lake Joe's Pond, and smaller body of water to the south Molly's Pond. (It's interesting to see how names get lost over time, because on my atlas Joe's Pond was labeled Jones Pond.)

Joe was so highly thought of that when he was an old man, the Vermont Legislature passed an act "granting relief to an infirm Indian by the name of

Joseph." A Mr. Hinman of Derby was provided $30 annually to look after Joe and provide for his necessities. Joe died in 1819 at the age of 79 and is buried in Newbury, Vermont, where his gun and canoe are preserved at the local museum.

When I was done with my reading I struck up a conversation with a smiling librarian who told me the building we were in also houses an opera house where the stage is on the Canadian side and most of the audience sits in the USA. She went on to explain that the building is a scaled-down replica of the Boston Opera House and is classified as a historic monument by both countries.

I turned our conversation to the neighborhood around the library, remarking that with several side streets connecting the two countries it would be impossible for customs to track all vehicles and pedestrians. "No so," she said, "there are sensors in the roads that activate cameras, and if a car that has entered the U.S. does not go into customs, customs goes to the car."

"What about someone on foot?" I asked.

"Same thing," she said. "The cameras pick up people crossing the border."

"How about me, I just walked from one side of the library to the other."

"They don't bother with the library, but if you were to walk out the door and cross into Canada, the Canadian Customs officials would know about it. I live nearby and at night I've seen people trying to sneak across the border in their car by turning the lights off and speeding but I think they got caught. They must be from the American side, because in Canada the vehicles are made so you cannot shut your lights off."

We continued our talk and she mentioned some houses are also straddling the border, and the people who live there have dual residency. "That can be an advantage," the librarian said, "because they can take advantage of which side is cheaper for certain things. For example you could register your car in Vermont and yet still get your health insurance in Canada. There's a street in Beebe, the next town to the west, where the houses on one side are in Canada and on the other side they are in the U.S. The street gets its name from the two countries, and is called Canusa Street. I have a friend that lives there and she says the people on the street tend to socialize with people from their own country, because the kids go to separate schools."

Later when I drove out of town heading to my cabin in north central Vermont, I wished I had dual residency. I'd have a fishing license for each country, and spend the weekends crossing back and forth in my quest for trout.

Snowshoeing in Northern Vermont
(Montgomery, Sheldon)

Old farmhouses dotted the landscape along the Missisquoi River and almost all of them had exposed wood showing through peeling paint.

Why don't these people ever paint their homes?" I asked my brother, Mark, now a Vermonter.

"I'm not sure they can afford to," was his reply.

He was probably right. Northern Vermont has more than its fair share of natural beauty, but it's tough to make a living off that. For every prosperous looking farm, there are three or four that appear like they are barely hanging on. A few others had given up the ghost and lay abandoned in the snowy fields. I'm rooting that the farmer's to make it, and I try to buy only produce and dairy products from New England to do my part. But my token gestures like mine may not be enough: half of all small dairy farms in New England have disappeared in the past ten years.

For people like me, who want to escape the crowds, Northern Vermont has a lot to offer, not the least of which is the stunning vistas made possible because of the rolling agricultural land. One encouraging development I noticed on my last trip was a recreation trail that runs for miles through the Northeast corner of the Green Mountain State. Starting at Saint Albans and angling northeast toward Richmond, the trail follows the bed of the Old Central Vermont Railway along the banks of the Missisquoi River. The trail is flat making it ideal for bicycling in warm weather and cross country skiing when the snow flies (you may have to share it with snowmobiles).

But Mark and I had snowshoes, not cross-country skis, and we were looking for deep woods. I'd been away from the mountains for a couple months and I yearned for hemlocks, spruce and fir rather than the oaks and pines around my home in southeastern Massachusetts. We soon found the type of terrain and trees I had in mind along the Trout River in Montgomery. We strapped on our snowshoes and off we went into the forest.

After a half hour of enjoyable tramping, I realized wearing snow pants or some kind of waterproof shell over my jeans would have been a good idea. With each step, the back of the snowshoe was kicking up wet snow onto the seat of my pants and before long it looked like I sat in a puddle. I thought I had packed everything into my backpack, even including a tiny foam pad to sit on when resting on a log or rock. But snow pants were not one of the items we brought along.

I also wasn't sure that my new light-weight snowshoes were the right size. Although the brochure said they were for adults who weighed up to 175, and the last time I looked I was 160, I was sinking in the snow a little deeper than anticipated. Either the manufacturers were wrong or I needed to get back on the exercise bike.

But the outing had its pleasant side. Strange ice formations had formed along a waterfall and animal tracks criss-crossed the woods: the delicate steps of a fox, the hops of a rabbit, and pigeon-toed waddle of a porcupine, dragging its tail of quills.

Of course the best part of any outing is the food, and we made a small fire and munched on our sandwiches. I felt especially healthy because instead of using cold cuts, Mark used ham-flavored "Soy Cuts" which were just as good as the real thing without nitrates and fat. However, even a porcupine sandwich would have tasted good after a couple hours of snowshoeing.

It was easy to see why cross-country skiing is declining and snowshoeing is booming. Snowshoeing is easy to learn and pleasantly aerobic. With crampons or spikes attached to the bottom, snowshoes will carry you over icy terrain without slipping as cross country skis do.

After snowshoeing we headed back to Mark's apartment where I took a hot shower, made a cup of tea and munched on dozens of chocolate chip cookies. There wasn't an ounce of Soy in the chocolate chip cookies but I figured I deserved a treat after the snowshoeing (just don't ask me to confirm my real weight).

Later we drove the back roads through the tiny village of Sheldon. We passed a sign which I thought I had misread.

"Am I seeing things or did that historic sign just say Civil War Action?" I asked.

Mark pulled the car over and sure enough the sign explained a bizarre Civil War event that occurred here. A small group of Confederate soldiers had gathered in Canada, and decided to give the North a taste of their own medicine after Sherman's raids through the South. The rebels infiltrated Saint Albans, Vermont, making frequent stops to reconnoiter the bank while hiding their true identity. When they figured they knew enough about the town they sprang into action, robbing the bank, and unsuccessfully trying to set the town ablaze. Then the Confederates high-tailed it out of town on horseback, galloping through Sheldon with a posse of Vermonters in close pursuit. From there, they made it to Canada, but half the stolen money was dropped on the way, and the raiders had little to show for their bold action.

New Hampshire

SOUTHERN & CENTRAL NH

Effort and Comfort: Mt. Monadnock and the Hancock Inn
(Jaffrey, Hancock, Peterborough)

Nestled among peaks and rivers, there's a group of small towns in the Monadnock Region of south-central New Hampshire that make for a restful yet interesting weekend destination by blending the past and the present.

We'd taken a long drive up in foul spring weather, trading highways for snaking two-lane roads that curve into the hills. Rain splashed on our windshield making the forest look like an impressionistic painting. We were only able to shake off the chill when welcomed at the 225-year-old Hancock Inn, situated on Main Street in picturesque Hancock NH. From the broad pine floors to the period décor, this inn personifies New England hospitality. Our suite included an electric fireplace that began to thaw us and a double Jacuzzi promised more relaxation after a drink and dinner. Because the weather continued to be foreboding, even walking across the street to sample other menus wasn't appealing, so the tavern and restaurant at the Hancock was a perfect solution.

The night we visited, a soloist entertained in the tavern as we enjoyed a giant bleu cheese burger and salad washed down with cold beer at the bar. The atmosphere was a genial mix of friendly service, local residents and visitors. The dining room offered a gourmet menu of lamb and local produce by a professional chef but these weary travelers were happy with the ambience of the tavern in the back of the building. Once the beer and food took hold, we were tempted to sing along with the guitarist in the corner, who crooned Pure Prairie League's "Amie," then van Morrison's and the Rolling Stones' older singles.

The suite at the front of the building is a generous size, with a sitting room, modern bath with shower and the aforementioned Jacuzzi alongside the giant four-poster bed. Period murals and stenciling adorn the walls and wingback chairs offer comfortable reading nooks where we pored over options for further exploration of the region. Innkeeper Marcia Coffin told us that part of the building was once the ballroom, and we learned that the music played for dancing there was amplified by "sounding glasses" hidden in the ceiling.

We peeked in unoccupied rooms to find a variety of individually-styled sizes and shapes in the accommodations, including one with a crochet canopy bed next to a claw-foot tub, the beautiful blue-and-yellow Rufus room and the wonderfully stenciled décor in a room with pencil post twin beds.

Marcia and her husband, Jarvis had made the transition from suburban Boston to the Inn just 18 months before our visit, immediately rehabbing bathrooms and moving the tavern from the front to the back of the building. "We always lived in old houses and did a lot of entertaining and were in the 'what next' phase when we saw the inn on the market," Marsha explained.

In the morning a sitting area on the second-floor landing offered make-your-own coffee while the old building slowly came to life. Hancock is a quiet town, its Main Street lined with historic buildings that must look much the way they did when Noah Wheeler opened the inn to travelers in 1789.

A fire was crackling in the tavern's hearth at breakfast, and the owner's golden retriever visited the dining room to greet everyone. Jarvis mustered up a hearty breakfast of omelets while Marcia refilled coffee and delivered sweet honey buns to each table. "Loving to cook is one way you get roped into inn keeping," she said of Jarvis's culinary skills. He had been the all-around cook early on, before a professional chef and sous-chef were hired for the sumptuous evening meals. We promised ourselves another visit, this time for dining and strolling the main street, before setting off on a day's adventure.

The location is perfect for a day's visit to the many attractions in and around Peterborough, including a basket weaving factory that allows public access, a park by the confluence of Nubanusit Brook and the Contoocook River, inns, restaurants, and a hike on nearby Mount Monadnock.

Try not to be deterred when the park rangers approach your car at the gate to Monadnock State Park.

"It's 30 degrees colder at the top, there are reports of sleet and the wind is blowing," one of them said to me with great foreboding when I arrived for a fall hike. "It will take you a minimum of two hours to get up and one-and-a-half to come down. It's going to be dark by 4:30."

The message doesn't quite mesh with the flood of people who attempt to scale the 3,160-foot mountain nearly every day; signs proclaim it the "Most Climbed" in North America, and it's known as perhaps the second-most-climbed in the world. That distinction is probably owed to its distance to Boston, approximately 60 miles away.

Indeed, if you could look down upon it from space, the "white dot" trail that goes most directly from the parking lot to the summit would look like

a busy ant mound on most summer days, a steady stream of climbers going higher and higher. Very closely paralleling it is the "white cross" trail that I always take coming down; it's no easier but seems that way because the bottom gets closer with every tired, muscle-aching step.

Once on the white dot trail, the rangers' warnings become clear. You walk through the woods for the first half-hour, but after that the trail quickly becomes a series of challenging scrambles up vertical rock faces. Because the 2.2 mile long white dot trail is most direct to the summit, it also means it's very steep. Trying to carry an injured or incapacitated hiker off this trail would be very difficult, making it better to scare off the unprepared before they begin.

While the hike is best described as strenuous, it can be a great achievement for novices. My children and nieces and nephews have been treated with snacks for reaching the top, an experience that they've earned despite much bellyaching over the climb. "Are we there yet" is a whine not limited to car trips!

As you approach the summit, the reward for your perspiration and aching joints (and crabby children, if they're still following you) becomes apparent. Views from the first, false summits reveal the fascination with mountain climbing the world over: look directly down into lakes and ponds, farm fields and green forests. Look distantly to see if Boston is visible today, turn to the north and west for beautiful blue-hued peaks. It's nearly the same view that Henry David Thoreau and Ralph Waldo Emerson climbed to enjoy (but there were fewer trees then!).

But then there is more. You may think you're almost done hiking when you're striding more easily over the bald rock of the peak above the tree-line, but getting to the actual summit takes more work. Continue following the trail, past rock cairns, over some streams and through a little stand of trees, across more rock and then even more. You'll have to scramble up the seams of bare granite to reach the smooth face of the summit, the concave peak at the very, very top. Here, hikers sit to recover and have a snack, ducking down out of the incessant wind. Best to have a jacket to put on, as the wind quickly cools you even before your legs have a chance to recuperate for the trip back down.

There are more ways to approach the summit than the white dot trail, and many are more gradual (and longer) ascents that can be done nearly year-round with the right equipment, such as the Pumpelly Trail. A group is developing a 50-mile trail linking Monadnock to Sunapee; we will add that

to our list of beautiful ways to experience New Hampshire in the future.
Hancock Inn:
www.hancockinn.com
 603-525-3318

On the River and In the Gardens
(Cornish and Charlestown)

The Cornish New Hampshire area can be explored the usual way by back roads, or you can add a little adventure and also experience the countryside by kayaking down the Connecticut River. Cornish is home to four of my favorite places: a beautiful stretch of rapids on the river, the Saint-Gaudens National Historic Site, the longest two-span covered bridge in the world, and the Chase House B&B. All are included in this trip.

Most of the Connecticut River flowing through central and southern Vermont and New Hampshire is placid water, with barely a discernible current. But the stretch that runs along the town of Cornish (and Hartland and Windsor on the Vermont side) has its share of rapids. There is one area that goes by the name of both "Hartland Rapids" and "Sumner Falls" that can be beautiful to look at but quite dangerous in high water. (It can be reached from the Hartland side of the river on a dirt road near where Route 5 crosses beneath Interstate 91.) Large shards of rock rise jaggedly from the river bottom and they are tough to spot in high water. Even in the summer when water levels are low these rapids can be tricky to negotiate. But just below them are more gentle stretches of fast water that will take you on a nice seven or eight mile paddle to the Windsor-Cornish covered bridge.

You can launch a canoe or kayak just below the biggest of the rapids at Sumner Falls, and let the current do much of the work as you glide down the river. Because the quick water adds oxygen to the river this is one area on the lower section of the Connecticut that holds trout in addition to smallmouth and largemouth bass. I've spent more than one voyage going down the river backwards in my kayak because I was so busy casting! Every now and then I'd peek over my shoulder just to make sure I wasn't heading directly toward a boulder in the middle of the river.

I always thought if I was in the stuck in the middle of the river I could get out in a shallow spot and have one leg in New Hampshire and the other in Vermont, but I've since learned that New Hampshire owns the river up to the high water mark on the Vermont side. If you search high enough in the woods along the Vermont shoreline you might even find some of the tall granite markers that delineate the two states. This boundary was permanently established in a Supreme Court ruling in 1933, and there's an old story about a farmer who thought the island he owned was in Vermont, but turned out to be in NH. "Thank God," he said, "I couldn't take another one of those Vermont winters." But maybe Vermont got the last laugh, because New Hampshire is responsible for bridge maintenance.

The river is not all that deep in spots, so if you do paddle in the summer, be sure to wear water shoes because you may have to drag your vessel over some rocks. But the effort is worth it, because most of the shoreline is un-interrupted forest, and soon you will be rewarded with a spectacular view of Mount Ascutney rising from the south. Further downstream my paddle ended at massive covered bridge, constructed in 1866. Incredibly the cost was just $9,000! The bridge is commonly called the Windsor-Cornish Cov-ered Bridge and it is the longest wooden covered bridge in the U.S. and the longest two span covered bridge in the world. This is a good spot to end your paddle and stretch your legs.

Route 12A parallels the New Hampshire side of the river, and a couple miles to the north is the Saint-Gaudens National Historic Site, once the resident of the great American sculptor Augustus Saint-Gauden. Approxi-mately 100 pieces of his work are either scattered on the grounds or inside the galleries at this location, including the Farragut Monument and my per-sonal favorite, the Shaw Memorial, depicting Robert Shaw and the 54th Massachusetts Regiment during the Civil War. Shaw is on horseback while his infantry is marching next to him in the 11 foot by 14 foot bronze cast sculpture. There is a fine attention to detail in the memorial – which explains why it took Saint-Gauden 14 years to complete!

The grounds at Saint-Gaudens are breathtaking, with views, paths through flowering plants and bushes, a mile-long woodland trail called the Blow-me-Down Trail that leads to a small mill pond. Near the Saint-Gauden home is a uniquely beautiful pathway that winds through sentinels of white birch. (The grounds are usually open year round, but the buildings are closed from November to Memorial Day.)

For your next day's exploration try heading south a few miles into Charlestown, New Hampshire to visit The Fort at Number 4, an exact rec-reation of a colonial fort located on the banks of the Connecticut River. The original fort was built in 1740, and it was the English colonists' north-ernmost outpost on the Connecticut River. This was during the ongoing French and Indian Wars that pitted the English colonists against the alliance of French and Indians of New England and Canada, and fort was a prime target of conflict because of its isolation. After you wander the grounds and see how difficult life must have been inside the fort be sure to read about the attacks that occurred there. One raid is particularly riveting, because it involves the captivity of Susanna Johnson, who left a detailed account of her experience, which included giving birth just two days into her captivity and forced march northwest to Lake Champlain and then on to Montreal. Whenever I read accounts like Susanna's it makes me realize I'm a cream-puff in comparison to the toughness of the people back in the Colonial days! We sure have it easy – so enjoy and appreciate the wonders along the Connecticut River!

North Star Canoe Rentals in Cornish:
www.kayak-canoe.com
603-542-6929. (Shuttle service is also available.)

Shaker Country
(Enfield and Lebanon)

People who march to a different drummer always interest me, and the Shakers of Enfield, New Hampshire certainly fit that description. In the mid 19th Century, Shakers lived in a thriving community that spanned 3,000 acres nestled along the shores of Mascoma Lake. Believing in communal ownership of property and equality of the sexes and the races, they strived to create heaven on earth. The only flaw in the "Shaker Way" as I see it was their vow of celibacy—not the best means of attracting new members or continuation of their culture into the future!

No matter what you think of their lifestyle, it is apparent they sure knew how to pick a good location for their village. With the gray-blue waters of Mascoma Lake to the northeast and the lush green slope of Mount Assurance to the southwest, the village has a certain serenity and beauty all its own. Dominating the village is the Great Stone Dwelling, an enormous granite structure built in 1841 that served as the spiritual and social center for the Shakers. Nearby are barns, shops, a mill, and various gardens and orchards.

One of the best ways to view the village is to walk up the gently sloping fields on Mount Assurance. After walking about a half mile you reach the Shaker Feast Grounds which were used as an area of outdoor worship. Today, the mountainside is preserved conservation land offering views of lake and village below, and laced with hiking trails.

On my visit to the area I stayed overnight at the Shaker Hill Bed and Breakfast, located on a ridge on the opposite side of the lake from the Shaker Village and Museum. One of the reasons I chose this particular inn was its sprawling country porch with rocking chairs. Another reason was the food. Innkeepers Nancy and Allen Smith offer hearty breakfasts such as blueberry pancakes or vegetable omelets. The inn dates back to the 1790's and all the rooms have been handsomely renovated. Especially interesting were the wide-board floors made from enormous pine planks. Some of the flooring came from ancient pines that in Colonial times were often referred to as "King Pines" because they were claimed by the King of England to make ship's masts.

Over breakfast at the inn, I talked with guests from three different parts of the United States; Oregon, Minnesota, and Ohio. Each had a different itinerary: one couple was heading west to visit Woodstock, Vermont and

Quechee Gorge, another guest was exploring Hanover, New Hampshire and Dartmouth College, and the third guest was looking to get some exercise. I recommended he rent a bicycle and ride the nearby Northern Rail Trail as I had done the previous year. The Northern Rail Trail runs from Lebanon, New Hampshire eastward through Enfield and continues on to Grafton, New Hampshire, spanning 23 miles. Winding through quiet countryside near Route 4 and adjacent to the Mascoma River, the trail was once a railroad line. Today it is covered with hard-packed stone dust, making it perfect for biking or walking.

If you were to start a bicycle ride in Lebanon and head eastward on the trail, you would cross the Mascoma River seven different times. Points of interest along the way are the kayak course on the river, views down Mascoma Lake to the Shaker Bridge, Mirror Lake with views of Mount Cardigan, and near its terminus is the Ruggles Mine on Riddle Hill Road. The trail is mostly flat, so even after a big breakfast at the Shaker Hill B&B, you should be able to cruise along and slowly burn off calories while enjoying some of New Hampshire's rural pleasures!

Shaker Hill Bed and Breakfast:
www.shakerhill.com
603-632-4519

Enfield Shaker Museum:
www.shakermuseum.org;
603-632-4346

Unusual New Hampshire and the Inn on Newfound Lake
(Bridgewater, Tilton, Northfield, Wolfeboro, Grafton, Warren)

Central New Hampshire has a some odd and unusual sites in picturesque country settings. When I set off to find them I was also looking for a centrally located B & B for my lodging and chose the Inn on Newfound Lake in Bridgewater. It was an easy choice for me because Newfound Lake, the fourth largest in the state, has been rated one of the purest bodies of water in the world. And best of all, the Inn has a huge veranda overlooking the lake, where you can sip a cocktail and watch the sun set over the lake's sparkling waters.

The inn dates back to 1840 when it was the mid-way stop on the stage route from Boston to Montreal. Its historic charms are still evident in the antique filled guest rooms, common sitting room and dining area. A touch of the modern world has been added with a Jacuzzi, exercise room and TV room. A large beach lies in front of the inn for swimming and boating in the warm weather months, while skating, snowmobile riding and snow-shoeing are popular in the winter.

I could have taken advantage of all the activities at the inn, but the lure of the road and some very unusual attractions were too strong to ignore. First stop was the Tilton Arch, just to the south in Northfield, New Hampshire. First time visitors who enter the town must do a double take at the huge granite arch that rises from a hilltop overlooking the town. Looking like the Arc de Triomphe, it was to be the memorial at the grave of local millionaire Charles Tilton. Unfortunately for Mr. Tilton and his huge ego, that part of town which was originally Tilton, NH became Northfield, NH and Charles Tilton did not want to be buried there. No matter, the site is not a graveyard anyways, and the millionaire could not be laid to rest there even if he wanted to.

The towns of Tilton and Northfield really are quite attractive, particularly an island park in the center of Tilton along its main road. A footbridge spans a small river leading to the island, and on the island itself is a bandstand where free concerts are held on Sundays in July and August. The island is great place for kids; I watched children wading in the rapids on the river while others were fishing from the banks. You may also want to stroll by the many Victorian buildings in town and visit the unique looking Tilton School

Library which was formerly the mansion of Charles Tilton, complete with strange markings on the wall of the reading room.

From Tilton, I decided to explore the back roads around Lake Winnipesaukee, and the highlight of that excursion was the Libby Museum in Wolfeboro, which houses everything from the weird to the wonderful, including lots of natural history exhibits. My favorite was the mountain lion skeleton next to a human skeleton: it drove home the point that mountain lions are actually a bit smaller than humans, something I was surprised at. This museum with all its oddities just might be the best little museum in northern New England, and children will love it.

My final stops were back in the direction of Newfound Lake, where I completed my long wandering loop drive. In Grafton, on top of Isinglass Mountain, is the "world famous" Ruggles Mine, with its tunnels and giant rooms to explore. Mineral collecting is allowed and you will find mica, amethyst, rose quartz and garnet.

In Plymouth, New Hampshire is another series of rock caves, this one called Polar Caves, formed when the glaciers knocked huge pieces of granite to the bottom of Hawks Cliff forming caves, nooks, and passageways. The Polar Cave Park is designed for families and it has kid-friendly walkways and exhibits.

Of all these natural and man-made oddities my favorite is in Warren. Author Joseph Citro in Curious New England describes this curiosity best: "Imagine you are stepping into an old-time science fiction movie…" He then goes onto to describe how you drive into the sleepy little village only to be shocked that a 70-foot missile pointed skyward from the village green. It's a Jupiter-C rocket, identical to the one that blasted Alan Shepard into outer space in 1961. And you thought all town commons have fountains or Civil War statues!

The Inn at Newfound Lake:
www.newfoundlake.com
800-745-7990

The Libby Museum:
Located on route 109 north of downtown Wolfeboro. Open seasonally,
June through mid-September.
603-569-1035

Ruggles Mine: open seasonally:
www.rugglesmine.com
603-523-4275

Polar Caves:
open seasonally.
603-536-1888

Castle in the Clouds, Squam Lake and Cheney House B&B
(Moultonborough, Holderness, Ashland and Groton)

I love a long Indian name, and Central New Hampshire has plenty of them: Pemigewasett River, Lake Winnipesaukee, Lake Waukewan, and so on. But I also like a good name in any language, especially one that conveys a sense of the place, and Castle in the Clouds fits the profile. Located on a promontory of the Ossipee Mountain Range in Moultonborough, Castle in the Clouds is a mansion built by millionaire Thomas Plant in 1913.

Now open to the public, Castle in the Clouds is managed and owned by the Lakes Region Conservation Trust, which also has thousands of surrounding rugged and wild acres under conservation protection. Trails criss-cross the woodlands, passing over rushing streams and beneath sweeping hemlocks, birch and maple, and occasionally offering views of the White Mountains to the north and Lake Winnipesauke to the southwest. Some visitors come just to tour the castle with its incredible craftsmanship and a handful of technological innovations of the early 20th Century, while others come for the hiking.

Another nearby attraction is the Squam Lakes Natural Science Center in Holderness, which will be of particular interest for families with children. It features the Gephart Exhibit Trail with live wildlife in trailside enclosures that include fox, fisher, bear, mountain lion, bald eagles, hawks, and owls. Squam Lake Boat Tours are also available through the Center, with one focusing on the lake's history beginning with the ice age and progressing through the Native American period, and into the present, including the filming of the movie "On Golden Pond" that occurred here. Another tour focuses on the lake's natural history, such as learning about loon behavior. In addition, the Center has a trail leading up to Mount Fayal which has great views of Squam Lake. Also on the property is a garden, called Kirkwood, featuring a variety of flowering plants that attracts butterflies and song birds.

On my visit to the area I stayed at a wonderful bed & breakfast, The Cheney House in Ashland, just a couple minutes drive from Route 93. The Cheney house was built in 1895, and the Victorian Home features incredible woodwork and cozy, comfortable rooms. Owner Bobbi Hoerter made me feel right at home, and I especially enjoyed the full gourmet breakfast she prepared. Because the Cheney House has only four guest rooms (each with private bathroom), you get that personal attention from Bobbi which is at the heart of the B&B experience. And it was clear she knew that the little things matter, such a refrigerator for the quests, a country porch with two easy chairs, cookies on the bedside table, and if you want to sleep late like I did; window shades that really block out the light.

The towns to the west of Ashland are not nearly as populated as those around Lake Winnipesauke and Squam Lakes, and during my trip I took a ramble on their country roads, first heading northwest past the northern edge of Newfound Lake, then following the Baker River on Route 25. Quiet roads, fields and forest grace the area. Nearby, just to the south, in the tiny little town of Groton, are geological features worth checking out at Sculptured Rocks Natural Area which has potholes eroded into odd shapes by waterborne stones.

Squam Lakes Natural Science Center:
www.nhnature.org
 603-968-7194

Castle in the Clouds:
www.castleintheclouds.org
603-476-5900

Cheney House Bed & Breakfast:
www.cheneyhouse.com
603-968-4499

An Inn on a Lake and Two Summits in the Clouds
(Sanbornton and Waterville)

Innkeepers Cindy and John Becker visited 70 inns for sale over a two year period before finally purchasing the Lakehouse at Ferry Point. We think all their time and research was well spent – the inn they now run is a real stand out. Few inns have their own lakefront but this one is on the shore of Lake Winnisquam and the view from the country porch alone is worth the trip. Kayaks, a gazebo and dock all beckon you to come down to the water's edge. But the comforts of the inn are difficult leave, especially the large den with a fireplace constructed of different kinds of stone from nearby Ruggles Mine. The ten bedrooms are all bright and airy, and most have a view of the lake.

One of the reasons we selected this inn is because that while it has a calming, country feel, it is only about a ten minute drive to Interstate 93, which makes it the perfect home base for outdoor activities. On our visit we set our sights on a hiking trail which makes a loop passing over two mountain summits and came highly recommended.

Many popular hiking trails in the White Mountains get busy on warm, sunny weekends. One is rarely alone on the trail during summer, regardless of how remote the location seems. And then there are a few like Welch-Dickey that are wildly popular and very busy. That doesn't mean it's not worth doing; it's one of our favorite hikes. In fact, we suggest avoiding the "leapfrogging" that is common on busy trails: when you pass a group, then stop to rest and they pass you, and on and on until you've heard enough of their conversations to know their family lineages.

To reach the trailhead take exit 28 off Interstate 93 and follow Route 49 toward Waterville Valley for 6 miles then turn left on Upper Mad River Road, then right on Orris Road to the parking lot. The parking lot was packed when we arrived and we decided to do the Dickey-Welch loop instead of the usual Welch-Dickey going in a counter-clockwise direction. Why not? This way, we passed many large groups coming down the mountain rather than waiting in line to climb through the tough spots. And there are more good reasons to try this tactic: we believe the trail is a little easier going clockwise. That may be perception and may not stand up to analysis, but we felt smart and energetic knowing we hadn't been passed by the church group, the school group, and the Boy Scouts that we encountered briefly along the way.

Now for the trail itself: on this hike, the journey is actually the destination. The distinguishing characteristic of this loop is the smooth, bare rock surface the trail crosses on the upper reaches of the mountains. This affords wonderful panoramic views, not just glimpses through trees. There's also an unearthly feeling when crossing yard upon yard of wide open, bare rock: where else does this occur, where the ground you walk on is uninterrupted, solid, smooth rock? It must be seen to be believed.

Hiking in our clockwise direction, there's about 40 minutes of wooded, moderate climbing before reaching the first awe-inspiring rock face on the south side of Mt. Dickey. In the steeper sections, you're aided by granite stepping stones lined up like flights of stairs. Yellow blazes can be tough to spot in some places; you may wander off-trail somewhat before realizing it, and the blazes painted on rocks are spaced at a distance that requires some patience and deliberate searching at times.

The first giant slanted rock is a promise of more to come, but when you reach the south-facing bare flank of Dickey the views are stunning, and a seat on the lip is a great break from which to consider the rest of the journey. Proceeding from there, you hit many broad expanses of rock with little oases of stunted spruce, fir and pine trees sprinkled on top. The rock plateaus are divided by small sections of woods. At the top of Dickey, the 360-degree views are splendid. Despite not being on the list of tallest peaks in the region, its nearly bald summit is indeed breathtaking, with blue-tinged peaks in every direction and, when we hiked, early yellows and reds of fall showing in the valleys.

Between Dickey and Welch the trail dips through a tough, steep, rocky gulley that requires some scrambling to complete. Here and on the other side of the Welch summit are undoubtedly the toughest segments of the trail. Those who are not capable of climbing over significant boulders or up very steep sections may similarly do the loop "backward" and enjoy Dickey, turning around halfway without significant danger. But you'd be surprised at the assumed ages of some of the mountaineers we saw coming through that challenging stretch. Impressive.

Welch's peak is similarly mostly bald, yet offers a respite from the wind in a rock-enclosed pit … if it's not full of lunching Boy Scouts, as when we were there. We enjoyed the solitude of an expanse of sunny rock on the opposite side of the summit, secluded by a clump of evergreens and cushioned by moss.

We munched on snacks while surveying our kingdom of greenery stretching for miles. It was a most satisfying snack.

Our afternoon descent of Welch was notable for the crowds. Lots of people like this hike. Too bad more don't do it backward and enjoy the solitude we experienced on our way up rather than filing one after another, looking always at the back of another person's head. We were the only hikers doing the trail in the clockwise direction. As we came off the mountain we passed through a lovely hemlock grove with mossy floor that felt ethereal and enchanted – if one isn't too tired to appreciate it. Also on this side of Welch, below the halfway mark, is a lovely brook with small cascades paralleling the trail.

In brief, Welch-Dickey (or Dickey-Welch, as we have described) is a wonderful moderate hike with some challenging sections on both sides of the Welch summit. The 4.4 mile loop took us about 4 hours with plenty of time for rest stops and photography. We've been on more difficult hikes with subpar views, so this is one to go out of your way for.

Lake House at Ferry Point:
www.new-hampshire-inn.com
603-524-0087

NORTHERN NEW HAMPSHIRE

Rivers of War, Rivers of Pleasure and Nootka Lodge
(Wells River, Vermont and Woodsville, New Hampshire)

Wells River, Vermont and Woodsville, New Hampshire both abut New England's longest river, the Connecticut. The two towns also share a link to our region's colonial past.

During the French and Indian Wars the area was the designated location for the Colonial Militia to meet Major Robert Rogers and his Rangers and escort them back to safety after their daring raid into enemy country. The Rangers were stationed at Fort Ticonderoga on Lake Champlain and under cover of darkness slipped past the French, and headed north up the lake. At the Missisquoi River they hid their row boats and trudged overland to the east until they reached the St. Francis Indian Village which was allied with the French. Rogers and his men surprised the villagers with an attack that was so sudden the entire village was destroyed.

While the raid was successful, the Rangers march back to the south and safety was not. Native warriors and French soldiers were hot on their trail, and Major Rogers was forced to split his men up into small groups to avoid detection. The strategy failed and many of the Rangers were killed in what is now the Northeast Kingdom of Vermont. The surviving Rangers, however, made it down to the Wells River confluence with the Connecticut, thinking they were "home free." But when they arrived they were devastated to find that the reinforcements who had been waiting for them had left and returned to the nearest Colonial fort (The Fort at Number Four in Charleston, over one hundred miles away. More Rangers died because of this dereliction of duty, but Major Rogers and several others did eventually reach the Fort at Number Four.

A few years later the exact same site played role in the Revolution, when George Washington commissioned the construction of a military road that was to go from the mouth of the Wells River northwestward into Canada. On this road, the plan was to have the Patriots march into Canada and make an offensive move against the British, much the same as Rogers had done against the Indians. The road, known as the Bayley-Hazen Military Road, was only partially completed, because Washington changed his mind thinking the British might use it to swoop south and attack northern New England.

Today, a visitor to the region would never know that this quiet back country played a role in two different wars. There are only a couple small signs and granite markers that commemorate the war-time exploits. A bridge spans the Connecticut River connecting the town of Wells River to Woodsville. Miles of dirt roads winding through farm country and hilly forests beckon the explorer. Besides the Connecticut River, anglers have a choice of fishing rivers in both states, such as the Wells River in Vermont or the Ammonoosuc River in New Hampshire. An especially scenic lake is Pearl Lake just east of Woodsville in Lisbon. Another interesting pond, where I saw plenty of moose tracks is Perch Pond in Lisbon.

Perhaps my favorite spot is two miles west of Woodsville on the Wild Ammonoosuc River. The atlas shows a covered bridge at a wonderful swimming hole labeled as the village of Swiftwater, but local residents refer to the spot as the "Big Eddy." Whatever name it goes by, the falls are beautiful. I recently discovered this spot while staying at the Nootka Lodge in Woodsville. Nootka Lodge is quite unique as it is made out of massive logs cut from Western Canada where the Nootka Indians live. The lodge is popular with snowmobilers in the winter because trails start right behind the lodge, but each season has its advantages, from fishing in the spring, swimming and panning for gold in the summer, and leaf-peeping in the fall. My reason for choosing Nootka Lodge was its convenient location. I'd go west and ramble around Vermont one day, while the next day I'd point the old Subaru east, and head up into the White Mountains.

One of my favorite outings was just a half-mile from the lodge, where I spent half a day hiking along the banks of the Wells River. Shaded by maples, hemlocks and pines, I followed the river past some old mill sites, traversed a beaver dam, and even caught a couple trout. It sure was hard to think that the river was connected with such brutality and hardship during the bygone days of Colonial New England.

Nootka Lodge:
www.nootkalodge.com
603-747-2418

Along The Ammonoosuc River & Sugar Hill
(Sugar Hill, Lisbon, Bath, Woodsville & More)

Franconia Notch State Park is a gateway to adventure, especially mountain climbing. But if you prefer biking, try heading north from the park on Interstate 93 and exiting at Franconia onto Route 117 heading west. This back road will lead you to the Ammonoosuc River Rail Trial and offer interesting stops before you arrive.

Just a few hundred feet down Route 117 stands New Hampshire's sole surviving blast furnace that transformed iron ore into iron. This stone octagonal shape structure sits across the Gale River. There is a small interpretive and picnic area by the side of the road where you can learn about the importance of these furnaces and how they contributed to the deforestation of New England in the distant past: their wood burning was one of the reasons why there are few old growth forests left.

Continue on Route 117 and you leave Franconia and enter the handsome village of Sugar Hill, home of Polly's Pancake Parlor on the right hand side of the road. It is a popular spot, even at lunch! Next you pass the tiny St. Matthews Church nestled beneath a sugar maple and white birch at a sharp bend in the road. (About 2.5 miles from the blast furnace.) You'll want to stop and take a picture especially if the hydrangeas are in bloom.

A short distance down Route 117, detour off to the left onto Sunset Hill Road, which has some great views of the White Mountains, and may make you start thinking of retiring in the North Country and having time to gaze at the sunsets in all seasons. Here you will find the Sugar Hill Sampler store, followed by the impressive Victorian Bed and Breakfast. A mile up the road is another choice for lodging, the Sunset House Grand Inn which is across from a golf course high up in the hills. Other inns in town include the Sugar Hill Inn, and the Hilltop Inn.

Back on 117, continue west, passing Harmon's Cheese Shop and Country Store, and then a short seven mile ride into Lisbon, where the Ammonoosuc River meanders and tumbles through a valley of farmland and forest. Our favorite access to the Rail Trail is at the intersection of Route 117 and Route 302, on River Road, a right hand turn. There is a small pullout where you can leave your car and hop on your bike and pedal on a trail that receives few visitors. The dirt and gravel trail is a total of 19 miles long, running from Littleton, through Lisbon and Bath, to its terminus at Woodsville. You will

want a mountain bike or a bike with fat tires to handle some of the large gravel chunks spread at swampy areas. (ATV's are allowed on the trail, but we've never seen one.)

By heading west on the trail (downriver) you first pass through meadows and farmland for about 4 miles before you reach Lisbon, where you could stop for a snack. Then the trail passes mostly through woods with glimpses of the river. If it's a hot day, there are some inviting pools to hop in for a swim. When the trail approaches Bath (about 5 miles from Lisbon) it offers a great view of the 345 foot Bath Covered Bridge built in 1832. Have your camera ready, because you can get a shot with the river, the bridge, and an iconic white New England church all in one picture.

After pedaling by the covered bridge you pass over the river on two long bridges, each offering good vistas of the river and the rapids below. We found one footpath down to the river and followed it to a deep pool where we could swim and fish. Nearby was a man panning for gold using both the old fashioned pan along with a modern hydraulic pump. He didn't find any gold and we didn't find any trout, but the setting made us feel like we were in Alaska with a gold-panner on one side of the river and an osprey screeching from a dead pine on the other. All we needed to make the spot complete was to see a moose, but none would oblige.

The remaining stretch of the rail trail to Woodsville is not as scenic as the section just described, so you may want to turn around here and pedal back to your car. More intrepid bikers can not only go on to Woodsville, but cross the Connecticut River and access the Montpelier & Wells River Trail into Vermont. It goes on and off road for 21 miles westward to Marshfield VT.

When you reach your car try completing a loop back to Route 93 by going west on Route 117 toward Woodsville and then turning left onto Route 112 to the Swiftwater Bridge. There is a large, beautiful swimming hole almost directly beneath the covered bridge on a branch of the Ammonoosuc called the Wild Ammonoosuc. To return to Franconia and Sugar Hill and Interstate 93, continue on Route 112 through a heavily forested area to its intersection with Route 116 and go northeast on Route 116 through the remote town of Easton until you reach Franconia.

Hard Hiking with a Soft Landing at Franconia Inn
(Franconia)

Hiking seems like an innocuous pastime. Strap on a backpack full of "rewards" for hauling your body along a trail and follow the blazes and cairns, right?

Well, that's not exactly what the Lafayette Ridge loop hike is like, as Alison learned. It's arduous. It's strenuous. And it's a reward in itself. Lafayette Ridge is one of New Hampshire's most beautiful trails, over some of the state's highest peaks. And it's not for the faint-hearted or out of shape. We suggest having a reservation somewhere close by as the post-hike reward (a hot bath, hearty meal and very few stairs to climb the next day will be of particular interest).

Alison and a partner in crime started early at the Bridal Falls parking lot in Franconia Notch State Park. It's clearly marked from Interstate 93. Just a few minutes into the rocky Falling Waters trail is a gorgeous 50-foot waterfall with just enough water flowing to provide a veil-like covering over the rocky face it cascades down. Enjoy the wonder and tranquility of it a few minutes because you may need that image to focus on as you ascend the steep trail to the top of Little Haystack Mountain.

Lafayette Ridge is New England's version of the Great Wall of China, the way it follows the spine linking the peaks of Little Haystack (approx. 4,700 feet), Lincoln (approx. 5,000 feet) and Lafayette (approx. 5,200 feet) mountains. The loop from Falling Waters, across the ridge, and down Greenleaf to Bridle Path, which takes you back to the parking lot, is nearly 8 miles, judged to take more than 5 hours (if you rest at the peaks to enjoy lunch or the view, add time). The views are unparalleled, the experience forever memorable. Due to its exposure above the tree line, the hike is not recommended in bad or threatening weather.

Without question, starting up Little Haystack on Falling Waters trail means getting the toughest part of the loop done first. If one were to ascend Bridle Trail to Greenleaf Hut and up from there it's a different story (open in season, about 3 miles in, the AMC hut is a good place for a break, to get water and use restrooms). Nobody says you have to do a loop, but we found that approach most satisfying, even if it's like eating your vegetables first.

Regardless of the direction you choose or whether you do a loop at all, the ups and downs over several hours takes a toll on your knees. Bring ibuprofen and plenty of water and energy bars.

Our choice for a post-hike reward was the Franconia Inn, just a few miles north on 93 through the Notch. An historic property in operation since 1863, it offers horseback riding and sleigh- or carriage rides in season. The grounds recall an era prior to asphalt and entertainment-centered resorts with flower gardens and wide grassy fields (in fact, a grass airstrip for small planes is just up the road).

The Inn offers all you need to unwind after a day on the trails: fine dining upstairs, a lovely screen porch with wicker chairs overlooking the pool and a basement pub and bar with adjacent game room. It's perfect for families with kids. The rooms we occupied shared an ample bathroom and overlooked the horse pastures. Accommodations are not deluxe, hermetically-sealed hotel units that we're used to: the atmosphere is old-New England with tiny staircases and rooms unlikely to have televisions. Still, the wing chairs, the quiet of the reading room near the front desk and other chintzy, grandma-like comfort were quite charming.

Having hiked in July, we opted for the outdoor pool to relax and unwind, followed by a drink and pub dinner in the basement. Hilarity ensued when we attempted ping-pong in our near-exhausted state, and we were glad driving wasn't part of the evening. While the big-screen television and library of movies was momentarily tempting, the beds were perfect for our needs.

Franconia Inn:
franconiainn.com
800-473-5299

Icy Adventure in the Whites: Lonesome Lake and Kinsman Ridge
(Franconia Notch)

For a "mountain man," Mike likes his hikes pretty flat -- and having his cooler of snacks nearby. Alison isn't afraid of heights, enjoying a vertical hike whenever possible. But she got a lesson in preparedness in mid-November when she set out to hike and was surprised to find snow at her destination, the Basin on Route 93 in Franconia Notch.

It shouldn't have been a surprise to find snow in New Hampshire in November; her brother, a veteran NH National Guard pilot, tells enough search and rescue stories to prove peak bagging ambitions make some people blind to the reality of being in the mountains. It's not the same as a video game and carrying a cell phone is not sufficient preparedness. And yet there she was, executing a hike she was less than 100 percent prepared for.

It was a business trip to Littleton that presented the opportunity for a solo hike in mid-November, when Alison succumbed to peak bagger syndrome, opting to try Kinsman Ridge, with opportunities to summit North and South Kinsman mountains, just south of Cannon Mountain. Having conquered Lafayette Ridge on the opposite side of Route 93, she hoped for some of the same spectacular views. What she got instead was a lesson in restraint.

Starting from Lafayette Campground near The Basin off Route 93, the Lonesome Lake Trail is pretty level and well-used. The lake itself is a beautiful spot about an hour up the trail if you're hiking casually. The Appalachian Mountain Club maintains a hut there year-round, offering rustic bathrooms and a place to refill your water if you're not staying the night. It's a favorite hike for families with kids.

When Alison set out there were several other hikers were en route, even before 8 a.m. on a cold morning. The snow on the ground was packed by many hikers, making it slippery and slow-going. With a budget of 5-6 hours, Alison believed she could cover a lot of territory. She planned to take the trail around the northern end of the lake, then turn right and head for Kinsman Ridge, turn south at the next junction (Kinsman Ridge Trail), and rapidly cover the next 3 miles, hitting North Kinsman peak. Only then would she have to consider if there was time to get to South Kinsman before descending to make her afternoon appointment in Littleton. It was not to be.

The snow on the ground was the primary reason Alison's plan could not be executed successfully, but there was more to it than that. For her, covering

8-10 miles in a couple of hours on flat ground is not difficult, but everyone needs to adjust calculations for elevation gain, and she did not do enough of that in her planning. It's not uncommon, even for people in good physical condition, to slow from their usual 4-5 mph walking pace to 1 mph in the mountains.

New Hampshire's high mountain trails aren't flat and smooth. When Alison hit the junction at Kinsman Ridge Trail at 9:30 a.m., she hoped to cover the 2.5 miles to Fishing Jimmy Trail junction in a little over an hour. Instead, it took two hours because she slowed down when she realized she was the only person on that trail that day (no other footprints in the snow). Twisting an ankle or falling on the ridge alone could be disastrous, and the snow was hiding many obstacles, including ice that had formed on many rocks. The ridge trail also had some unexpected surprises in the form of snow-covered ladders in places where the terrain was too steep to scramble. Even a significant amount of research and planning may not reveal all of the things that can thwart a plan, so flexibility is important. As Mike tells audiences who come to hear his "survival" presentations, sticking to a plan can be the worst decision to make.

Another unexpected disappointment was Kinsman Ridge Trail's lack of spectacular vistas. Unlike Lafayette Ridge, which runs along the spine of a ridge above the tree-line, this trail is deep in the forest with only an occasional glimpse northward to Cannon and Washington. Alison plowed along, going north-to-south, thinking that she'd get a chance to snap some great photos when she reached the peak, but that never happened.

Decision time came at 11:30 a.m. when Alison reached the junction of Kinsman Ridge and Fishing Jimmy trails, four hours into the hike. It had been a much slower trip than anticipated, and she had to acknowledge that she was likely to continue hitting challenging terrain. From there it's at least 3 miles back to Lafayette Campground by the most direct route, so instead of peak bagging she had to bag going to the peak. The upper end of Fishing Jimmy trail was no picnic either, with many slippery rocks (this time descending); prompting her to hope nobody saw the graceless sliding-spinning-splitting moves and grab-a-tree-for-dear-life tactics that got her through the worst of it.

From now on, traction devices called micro spikes will be part of Alison's hiking gear, and those trekking poles that she dislikes will be required equipment. Both would have made a difference in her stability under the slippery conditions.

When she hit the convergence of trails at the Lonesome Lake hut, the area was swarming with families enjoying the view, and perhaps setting out for their own hike in the sun. It was a good time to pause, snap a photo and enjoy the accomplishment of doing a significant number of miles in the snow, peaks or no peaks.

Weeks State Park
(Lancaster and Whitefield)

Congressman John Wingate Weeks of New Hampshire played an important role in preserving some of our favorite forests here in New England. In 1911, Weeks sponsored legislation to create National Forests in the Eastern United States. The resulting Weeks Act allowed the Federal Government to buy the White Mountain National Forest.

Besides this important environmental step, Congressman Weeks also had an eye toward beauty, building his summer home on Mount Prospect in Lancaster, New Hampshire in 1912. His family later donated the entire 420 acre estate to the people of New Hampshire, and today the mountain and its historic home are open to the public. The views from the summit of Mount Prospect are tremendous—on clear days you can gaze to the east and see Mount Washington and the Presidential Range. An observation tower allows visitors a panoramic vista but also serves as an active fire lookout. (If the summer lodge is open, ask the ranger if you can take a peek at the second floor reading room. Mounted on the wall is the head of an enormous bull moose. The moose was shot by Theodore Roosevelt and given to Mr. Weeks.)

Your options for reaching the mountaintop include driving on the Mount Prospect Scenic Byway (seasonal) or hiking to the summit on the Heritage Trail and Old Carriage Road path. This trail can be accessed from Reed Road, about .3 miles from Route 3 on the north side of the mountain. The Heritage Trail within the park is just a fraction of the 230 mile New Hampshire Heritage Trail which runs from Massachusetts to Canada.

Although Old Carriage Road is too steep for cross-country skiing or hikers who prefer gentle slopes, the park does have a beautiful multi-use trail, called the Mountain Loop Trail, which runs for three miles around the base of Mount Prospect. The trail passes through stands of white spruce, white cedar, sugar maple, beech and ash. While the Mountain Loop Trail does have its hilly sections, the rises and falls are moderate, and there are a couple areas offering views of surrounding mountains. In the spring, wildflowers are abundant along the path, while in the fall hikers are treated to the rich hues of autumn foliage and perhaps a migrating hawk or two.

To increase your odds of seeing hawks ride the thermals, there is rocky outcrop near the mountain's summit, which offers good views to the north – the direction from which the hawks are coming from. The trail to this lookout begins just behind the summer lodge at the mountaintop. Most raptors head south for the winter, but the red-tailed hawk is a year round resident, and can often be seen perched on a branch of a dead tree surveying the area for any sign of movement and a potential meal.

If all the hiking at the mountain has you as tired out as I was, you might want to treat yourself to a night at the Spaulding Inn in neighboring White-field, New Hampshire. On my visit, I was immediately impressed by the inn because of their wide country porch and rocking chairs. Inside the inn features a one-of-a-kind children's room, a comfortable reading room, and a restaurant. The inn is family owned and operated, and guests are made to feel right at home. It is a quiet, peaceful spot, surrounded by 210 protected acres of forest and meadows.

Weeks State Park Association offers a wide range of educatioal programs. The park's telephone number is 603-788-4004.

A Weekend at Pinkham Notch and the AMC Lodge
(Pinkham Notch)

At the Appalachian Mountain Club's Pinkham Notch Lodge, an outdoor enthusiast can spend the day exploring the White Mountains and find comfortable accommodations waiting at nightfall. Situated just a few miles north of North Conway, New Hampshire, Pinkham Notch lies at the eastern base of Mount Washington, New England's highest peak. While more experienced hikers test their skills on Mount Washington, families with young children can explore dozens of trails that lead to waterfalls, swimming holes, hilltop views, and unique geological features. Best of all a weekend at Pinkham Lodge won't break the bank and seems a world away from the consumerism and traffic that has smothered North Conway.

Two great family hikes begin right across the street from the lodge. The Square Ledge Trail climbs about 400 feet to a granite ledge with a spectacular view of the notch and Mount Washington beyond, especially scenic in the autumn when the hills are ablaze with color. Although the round trip hike is only about an hour, the last 100 feet of the trail involves a steep uphill climb, giving a young hiker a modest challenge. And when they reach the summit after this workout they have a real sense of accomplishment as they look down at the notch and across at the mountains, many of which jut into the clouds.

White birch are scattered along the trail adding color to your walk, and wildlife from ruffed grouse to small toads are often seen along the way. The highlight of the walk to the ledge is Hangover Rock, a large cave-like shelter beneath an overhanging piece of granite. Kids will love this shelter, where their imagination can conjure up scenes of Native American huddled around a fire beneath the protective outcrop of rock.

The Lost Pond Trail (part of the Appalachian Trail) is also across the street from the Lodge, but is a very different hike from Square Ledge. Rather than climbing a mountain side, this trail first follows the Ellis River before veering to the southeast where it leads to Lost Pond, a remote pond in a forest of hardwoods and balsam fir. The pond has a colony of beaver, which can often be seen in the late afternoon or early morning. Look for them coming and going from their lodges, carrying branches and foliage to their lodge on the opposite shoreline. There is also a good view across the pond of Mount Washington, Huntington Ravine, and the Gulf Slides. Because the trail is primarily flat it's a good choice for snowshoeing or cross-country skiing in the winter.

My daughter and I hiked this trail after enjoying the view at Square Ledge, and we stopped for a rest at a deep pool in the crystal clear Ellis River. It was here that we met a "thru hiker" trekking the Appalachian Trail. Tyler Jones (trail name Tippy Canoe) had been walking the trail alone since spring when he left Georgia on his way to the northern terminus at Mount Katahdin. We talked for awhile about life on the trail, and the little adventures encountered along the way.

Tyler described how he had an exciting encounter with a bear and her cubs on the trail in New Jersey. While Tyler was on the trail the bear came down out of the forest and parked itself on the path. Tyler stopped, began to remove his pack to get his camera, but then froze when three cubs ambled out of the woods. The bear then took a few steps toward him, and gave a loud woof, which sent the cubs up a tree and Tyler's heart pounding. Tyler stood perfectly still and the bear stationed herself on the trail, apparently contemplating whether the human constituted a threat. Then the bear woofed again, the cubs scrambled out of the tree, and the four-legged family went back up the hill, leaving Tyler to wonder how close he came to being charged.

After hikers work up an appetite on the trail, they try to make it to the Lodge at six o'clock sharp, when a family style dinner is served. The food is excellent and there is plenty of it. Dinner offers you a chance to meet other explorers, and children quickly make friends with fellow hikers as they talk about what mountains they climbed. (A buffet breakfast is also served.) Some evenings after dinner, programs, such as slide presentations, are held at the lodge. Other nights, folks gather around the stone fireplace, and recount the day's events and share suggestions for future explorations. With a full day of outdoor activity completed, most everyone hits the sack by ten o'clock. The rooms at the lodge are spartan, with twin bunk beds, and a common bathroom is shared. But these simple accommodations come with a low price, about half what you would pay at a hotel. Both private rooms and common bunkrooms for up to five guests are available.

For more ambitious hikers, the AMC has eight "high huts" for lodging. These smaller lodges are scattered in the White Mountains and are accessible only by foot. They range from Galehead at a 3,800 foot elevation with rugged hiking, to Lonesome Lake at 2,700 with easy hiking. Lonesome Lake Hut is a great family destination where guests stay in two separate bunkhouses with various size rooms. Natural history hikes and activities are scheduled daily. Dinner and breakfast are available.

Experienced hikers often spend considerable time on the trail, walking hut to hut, where the ridge line offers spectacular views and the hiking is challenging. But even with difficult terrain, the hut system makes hiking that much easier, because tents and cooking items can be left behind.

Whether you skills run from beginner to expert, a hike in the "Whites" combined with the AMC huts, let you enjoy the mountains by day and new friends and shelter at night.

AMC Reservations:
www.outdoors.org
603-466-2727
You can stay at the huts and lodge without being an AMC member,
but membership allows discounts on lodging rates, workshops, and many other
benefits. Besides the Pinkham Lodge, there is roadside lodging at the AMC's
Crawford Hostel at Crawford Notch.

Other trails that depart near Pinkham Lodge include:
Crystal Cascade (.7 mile round-trip walk to waterfall)
Lowe's Bald Spot via Old Jackson Road (4.2 mile to overlook)

Other favorite walks near North Conway include:
Diana's Bath, West Side Rd, North Conway (short walk to waterfalls--great
for swimming--expect many other visitors) Glen Ellis Falls, 9 miles
from Jackson on Route 16 (a half mile walk to a 60 foot waterfall)
Rocky Gorge, Kancamagus Highway (easy walk along the Swift River)

Exploring the Wilds of the Androscoggin River
(Errol and Cambridge)

I'd never gone trout fishing with a guide before, so I jumped at the chance when my friend Ed invited me to join him on a drift boat with guide John Howe. I was even happier about my decision when we arrived at the upper reaches of the Androscoggin River in New Hampshire. The river was running high, with dark black waves rolling over submerged boulders--not the kind of water to fish from a canoe. (I later learned that the river was running unusually high for summer. In a more typical year the section below the Mollidgwock Campground is enjoyed by canoeists who can handle Class I-II whitewater. Anglers can also wade the river at a number of pull-offs.)

We launched just below the village of Errol at dawn, and I quickly realized just how well suited a drift boat is for this river. Waves that would terrify me in a canoe were handled with ease by Howe, and the drift boat gently glided over them. The boat was so steady in fact that we could stand in the bow and cast while bobbing through rapids.

Another pleasant realization was that Howe fit my idea of what a good guide should be. He obviously knew the river, the fish, and the art of fly fishing, but it was the way he shared his knowledge that made the float so enjoyable. Rather than overpower you with advice or dictate instructions, Howe sprinkled his tips at intervals, letting the beauty of the river be the focal point of the trip rather than himself. I asked him how he got into the business and he explained that as a kid he would go on camping trips with his family in the Rockies, learning to fly fish at a young age. Later, he followed his passion to be outdoors, becoming a land surveyor, fly fishing instructor, and guide. And today, he was clearly enjoying himself, working the oars to keep us on course and occasionally dropping anchor at a choice location.

"Don't pass up any water," offered Howe, "we've caught nice fish in the middle of rapids as well as quiet eddies." And so Ed and I took turns casting from the bow into all kinds of water. Our first fish was a small Atlantic salmon that cleared the water like a rocket, and surprised me with its strength. Then came a brookie from a shaded pool near shore, followed by a nice sized rainbow taken from white water. Minutes later a brown trout that was holding just behind an island hit Ed's Alder fly imitation. I looked at my watch: we had been on the river half an hour and had caught four species of game fish.

I asked Howe if this was common. "Every trip is different, but we almost always catch fish. Usually they range in size like they have today, from 10 inches to 13 inches, but every now and then someone hooks into something more substantial. Last year we landed an 18 inch brook trout and a six pound brown in the same week. We release all the fish we catch to keep the fishing first rate."

The size of the brook trout surprised me, but not the brown. Don Miller, a fisheries biologist for northern New Hampshire with the New Hampshire Fish and Game Department, had told me about the Androscoggin's legendary browns and rated the river as perhaps the best in the state. The big browns often stay in the deep holes by day, then venture out for nocturnal forays, especially holding to this pattern in July and August. Some of the holes in the river are over thirty feet deep, and occasionally a lucky angler who drifts a fly near the bottom feels the jarring tug of an Androscoggin brown.

As our boat bobbed along, I settled back and enjoyed the ride. The river flows due south here, through an area known as the Thirteen Mile Wilderness, before turning east at the town of Gorham and heading into Maine. On our left was a jagged ridge of spruce and fir, while to the right Route 16 parallels the river. There are no homes or stores to mar the scenery. I knew there were plenty of moose nearby, because that morning we saw a cow and calf cross Route 16 near our launch site.

The Androscoggin is one of New England's major waterways, rising in Lake Umbagog and flowing 167 miles to the Atlantic through Maine's Merrymeeting Bay. The case could be made that the true river is much longer, and that the Magalloway River and Androscoggin are actually one long river. If you look on a map you will see that the Magalloway River flows into Umbagog at a spot quite close to where the Androscoggin leaves the lake. Whatever its true length, this upper stretch of the river is a true gem.

Farther downstream, where the river turns toward Maine, the Androscoggin is still cleansing itself of the dioxins released into the river by the paper mills. (Dioxin is a byproduct of chlorine used to bleach paper.) Progress is being made in the fight against pollution, such as a recent pact in Maine to reduce the discharge of dioxin to the point where fish in the river will be safe to eat in four years. More immediate progress is evidenced by the announcement that the 15 mile stretch of river from the New Hampshire state line to Sunday River is now deemed swimmable. Even the pristine upper stretch that we were floating had its problems from the logging industry.

"At certain times of the year it was impossible to see the surface of the water as thousands of cords of pulpwood stretched for miles from bank to bank," writes author Page Jones in her book *Evolution of a Valley*. "From time to time log booms strung across the river on steel cables separated stretches of water above the rapids so that pulpwood could be released as needed at the mills downstream at Berlin."

It's hard to imagine this stretch of water being anything but the way it is now: beautiful and wild. And there are more rivers to the north that are just like it, offering the explorer a life-time of weekend trips of fishing and canoeing. Louise Dickenson Rich, sang their virtues and those of the surrounding lakes in her 1942 book *We Took to the Woods*, "Kennebago to Rangeley to Cupsuptic down they drop, level to level, through short snarling rivers: Mooselukmeguntic to the Richardsons to Pond-in-the-River, and through Rapid River to Umbagog, whence they empty into the Androscoggin and begin the long south-easterly curve back to the ocean. I like to say their names, and I wish I could make you see them--long, lovely, lonely stretches of water shut in by dark hills."

Morning stretches into noon, as we roll down the river, landing small fish but not the lunker browns that rule the depths. Stretches of fast water and smooth glides run one after the other, and the only sound is the low murmur of the river itself. A great blue heron rises from the shore and lazily flaps its way down river. We follow, Jon pulling on the oars primarily for steering, rocking over rapids and drifting like a fallen leaf through the flat water. Soon we begin to catch smallmouth bass, which put up a mighty fight, bulldogging down to the depths then breaking the surface in an effort to free the hook. Like the trout, we catch them in all kinds of water, but the bigger ones come when we drift muddler minnows into deep pools.

After lunch we fish a little more, but the sun has put the trout down, and our casts are half-hearted. But the river entertains us with its waves, colors, and motion and I feel like following it to the sea. Some day...

That night, long after I'm off the water, when I'm just about to drift off to sleep, I still feel like I'm in the boat, gently rising and falling over waves. I replay the fight of a rainbow, see the spruce and fir roll by, and imagine I can smell that wonderful river scent of flowing water. A river can stay with you a long time.

Guide Service
John Howe guides on both the Androscoggin and the Connecticut River.
He is at Tall Timber Lodge:
www.talltimberfishing.com
603-538-9589

Bald Eagles on Lake Umbagog
(Errol)

Straddling the Maine-New Hampshire border, Lake Umbagog beckons the explorer with its 50 miles of wild shoreline. My fishing pal Ed and I had no illusions about exploring it all in a weekend trip, so we set our sights on something we had never seen before--a nesting bald eagle.

With the aid of an electric motor mounted on the back of our canoe we made good time covering the three miles of the Androscoggin River that ran between our launch site, just off Route 26, and the lake. (One could launch directly into Lake Umbagog, but there's something adventurous about entering a lake from a river. It's also the quicker way to see the eagles nest which is situated near where the Androscoggin exits the lake.) On our way upstream we made frequent stops, poking into back water sloughs where we scared up a common merganser, a female with crested brown head and pure white throat. What a handsome bird, large and sleek, and as adept at chasing down fish as a loon. Other birds took flight as we explored the marshes, such as night herons, ring-necked ducks, a great blue herons and a wood duck.

While cruising upriver we trolled two lines behind the canoe, but evidently there were few fish in this stretch or the mergansers had got to them first. Even though the current was slow, the motor helped offset a brisk the wind that came right down the river directly at us. With the motor angled to one side we were able to paddle on the other, doubling our speed, for the final mile to lake. Then with the lake in sight, framed by blue green mountains, we cut the motor and paddled the rest of the way. I was glad we did, because we were greeted by the mournful wail of a loon, then minutes later by the screech of an osprey.

The lake is a big one, sprawling some 7,800 acres in a generally north-south direction, with plenty of islands and coves for exploring. Its waters, however, are relatively shallow, supporting yellow perch, smallmouth bass, and lake chub, with salmon, brook trout and browns in the northern section of the lake where there are some deep holes. Umbagog even has a floating island held together by roots of grasses, shrub-wood and bushes that changes locations in the marshy area near where the Androscoggin leaves Umbagog.

Surrounding the lake is some of the most diverse habitat in New England; flood-plain forests of silver maple, red maple and elm, swamps with uncommon white cedar, and bogs filled with sphagnum moss, Labrador tea, tama-

rack, and carnivorous pitcher plants. Along rockier part of the lake shore are jack pines, a relatively rare tree in New Hampshire and Maine. Thankfully much of the shoreline is protected within the Lake Umbagog National Wildlife Refuge, a mixture of private and public lands established as a refuge in 1992. As wild as the shoreline is, it's still easily accessible to boaters, with a launch site at the southern end of the lake as well as access from the Magalloway River or the Androscoggin. Thirty primitive campsites are scattered about the lake on its shoreline and islands. We noticed one campsite on an island not far from the Androscoggin that looked like an especially good spot.

We stopped paddling and let the peace of the place sink in. So much greenery around us, a Westerner would think they were in a jungle, especially if they glided into one of the narrow coves. The lake lived up to my expectations as a wild place, and already, Ed and I were planning a return trip, one where we would cross the lake (wind permitting) to the famed Rapid River, and explore it by foot. The Rapid River (on the Maine side of Umbagog) plunges for about two miles from its outlet from Pond in the River at the lower end of Lower Richardson Lake. Known for its salmon and native brook trout, sections of the river are carefully managed with fly-fishing only regulations, catch and release for the trout, and a one salmon per day limit prior to August 15 and catch and release after that date. When I told Ed how the river occasionally gives up salmon over 23 inches and brook trout over four pounds, he almost hopped out of the canoe and swam over. But Umbagog's a big lake, and there was no way we could explore the Rapid and motor back in a day. And like all lakes in the North Country a crossing is not to be taken lightly, winds can kick up at suddenly and canoeists are especially vulnerable.

The eagles nest we had come to see is near the mouth of the Androscoggin and the end of the Magalloway River that meet in a confusing configurations of narrow channels and marshy setbacks known as Leonard Pond, which is not a pond at all. We located the Magalloway and paddled upstream a short distance to a good vantage point for viewing the nest. Located near the top of an enormous dead pine, two eagles stood guard over the nest, one directly on it and the other at the very tip of the pine. On such a perch they could see for miles, and silhouetted against the crystal blue sky the eagles, with white heads gleaming, looked like royal monarchs surveying their kingdom of woods and water. Seeing the eagles made us forget all about the Rapid River salmon.

We waited with another canoe, behind a roped off area near the eagle's pine tree, hoping we would see one glide off so we could see its six-and-a-half-foot wingspan. But both the male and the larger female were content on their perch, no doubt scanning the water for a fish that might break the surface. Although they can grab a fish by swooping down and skimming the water with their black talons, eagles prefers to scavenge for dead fish or carrion rather than hunt. At Umbagog, with its healthy population of ospreys, the eagles can steal their food as well, harassing an osprey on the wing until it drops its catch which the eagle will catch deftly in mid-air.

The nest was large and coarse, comprised of sticks, turf and pine needles as a liner, and each year more material is added, with some nests becoming enormous affairs. Eagles mate for life and will use the same nest year after year, although this pair had previously set up housekeeping on the other side of the lake, and so one never knows which side of the lake they will be on. One to three eggs are laid, and an incubation period of about 30 to 35 days follows with the female sitting on the nest while the male brings her food. When the young hatch both parents share in the feeding. By the tenth or eleventh week from hatching the young will take their first flight on their way to becoming masters of the sky.

Appreciation of the majesty of eagles was not always evident, especially when the birds were blamed for loss of livestock and game animals. They were even accused of carrying off small children, and the birds were trapped, shot and poisoned. Their decline however had more to do with loss of habitat and the use of pesticides, particularly the widespread use of DDT in the 1950's and 1960's. Other predators at the top of their food chain, such as ospreys and peregrine falcons, also were harmed by the "miracle" pesticide. DDT would be washed from farmers' fields into lakes and rivers where it was absorbed in the tissues of tiny plants and animals, which would be consumed by fish. The birds of prey who subsisted mainly on fish were receiving a highly concentrated dose of the chemical, which inhibited their capacity to produce calcium. When the birds laid their eggs, the shells were soft, and populations declined in alarming proportions. Finally DDT was banned in 1972.

While Ed kept an eye on the eagles, I scanned the atlas, noting how the Magalloway came down into Umbagog from sections of New Hampshire so remote they didn't even have a town name, but rather were Grants, such as Second College Grant and Dix Grant. What an area to explore! The Dead Diamond River and the Swift Diamond River were filed away in the memory bank for future hikes. Even this lower stretch of the Magalloway looked like a great place to see wildlife, running through forest and marsh for a couple miles between the lake and Route 16. So we paddled up the river, enjoying more bird life. A merganser scolded us, a kingbird harassed a blackbird, and a kingfisher plunged into the river for a meal. We watched a mink prowl the shoreline, darting in and out of the brush, flushing a red-winged blackbird that escaped in the nick of time.

Farther up the river we went, expecting to see a moose each time we rounded a bend. Instead, we were surprised when three men came cruising down the river in a strange looking, home-made steam boat! It was a tiny little contraption; the furnace and steam pipe took up most of the boat, with the men crowded in the back.

"Does she burn wood?" I asked.

"Yup, and just about anything else we feed her," came the reply.

"Steam powered, right?"

"Yup, and moves pretty good too."

"What's its name?"

"It's called 'I Did It' -- not to be confused with Idiot."

Maybe it's not as wild as Alaska, but there's room up here for all types.

Launch Sites On Androscoggin River to Reach Lake Umbagog
From the center of Errol, on Route 26 heading southeast, just after cross-ing the Androscoggin River, is a dirt road that leads north about a mile to a launch site into the river. From here it's a three mile paddle up-stream to the river. Another option, if you want to cut off some paddling time is to put-in off Route 16, just north of Errol. There is no official boat launch so look for parking on the shoulder of the road where allowed.

On Top of the World and Tall Timber Lodge
(Dixville Notch and Pittsburg)

Table Rock has an elevation of 2,500 feet, offering commanding views of the rugged mountains that form Dixville Notch. Unlike many climbs in the White Mountains, Table Rock is a relatively short one, with two trails to choose from. Both trails begin on Route 26 opposite the Balsams Resort, just west of Dixville Notch State Park. The Table Rock Hiking Trail is about a 2 mile round trip hike with a gradual ascent to the summit, and the Table Rock Climbing Trail is only a half mile round trip, but like the name says this is a climb, where you have to use your hands as much as your feet. I figured I'd test the old knees and see if they could make the climb.

After 5 minutes my legs ached, after 10 my arms were felt like dead weight, and at 15 my heart was hammering so loud I couldn't hear the birds. Finally I rested, and realized this climbing trail is about as direct an approach you can make on Table Rock without using ropes.

But fifteen more minutes of effort brought me to a most incredible view. To the west you can gaze into Vermont, directly below is Lake Gloriette, and to the east is Dixville Notch with Route 26 snaking through the chasm toward Lake Umbagog. For an even better vista, one could creep out onto a shelf of rock that juts out over the cliff. I started out carefully, immediately opting to creep on hands and knees for fear of falling off, and then to a commando crawl on my belly. Call me a chicken, but this chicken knows it can't fly.

Dixville Notch is different than the other notches in the Whites, as it has a sharp, jagged profile rather than a smooth one like those in the just a few miles to the south. Geologists theorize that the rocky crags of Dixville Notch were formed 500 million years ago, making these among the oldest rocks in the state. From the top of Table Rock, you can look out on the ledges of Mount Abanaki, where peregrine falcons (the fastest birds in the world) nest.

After I retraced my steps and returned to my car, I glanced up at the mountains. Clouds casting shadows that made the forest appear almost black. From such a distance the trees themselves appear to be a single, uniform conifer, but if you climb these hills you discover a wide mix of conifers, tending to be segregated by elevation. In the lowlands, balsam fir, white cedar and the graceful tamarack, which sheds its needles, grow along backwoods swamps. As you climb to higher ground the white spruce and hemlocks will be scattered among the hardwoods, giving way to red spruce and then ultimately black spruce and the widespread balsam fir near the exposed mountain tops and tree line.

While I find hemlocks, tamaracks and cedars easy to identify, I need time to distinguish the spruces from the firs if I'm deep in a forest. But from a car, where I can see the crowns of trees, identification is easier because the balsam fir has a compact crown that tapers to a point while the spruce is looser and broader. Whenever I drive to the North Country from my home in southern New England, I try to look for the "north woods line" where the oaks and white pines begin to give way to the spruce and fir, as if giving the traveler an official welcome to the wilder country of moose, fisher, and bobcat.

When winter rolls in I don't try and tackle Table Rock, but instead prefer to snowshoe in the lower elevations of Dixville Notch, such as areas near the Balsams or along the Mohawk River. When it comes to snowshoeing my rule of thumb is that the snow should be over six inches deep, which it usually is this far up in the White Mountains. Snow amounts under six inches usually means that snowshoeing is expending more effort than merely hiking, and I recommend putting on a pair of warm boots and taking to the trails on foot.

When I'm exerting myself in cold weather I try to wear a polypropylene long underwear shirt which wicks away moisture from your body, unlike cotton and wool that trap your body's sweat, causing you to become chilled the moment you stop exercising. Equally important is to wear layers, so that you can shed the outer layers and put them in your pack while snowshoeing or hiking, and then put them back on if you stop for a rest. And remember to bring plenty of water to drink because that vapor you exhale is water, and you've got to drink often, or you will become dehydrated without even knowing it. Because you are burning calories rapidly, pack plenty of high energy snacks, such as fruit or a candy bar. My favorite trail snack is M&M's mixed with peanuts and raisins.

Wearing a hat should be second nature in the winter, because of the heat loss that can occur from a bare head. And in really cold weather the hats that pull down into face masks work great in guarding your skin from punishing winds. A good pair of mittens keeps your hands much warmer than gloves, because within the mittens all the fingers help to generate "communal warmth." And don't forget to stretch before hitting the slopes or trail.

While many folks take to the trails in summer or fall with very little preparation and carrying little gear, winter is less forgiving in northern New

Hampshire. With fewer fellow hikers on the trails, you may find yourself quite alone if you run into trouble.

Pittsburg, NH is another great are to snowshoe. The 400 mile long Connecticut River originates here, at a small beaver pond on the Canadian border, and the country is rugged and wild. Much of the forest in the region is owned by paper companies, which allow exploration on the miles of logging roads that crisscross the woods.

Tall Timber Lodge, located on the shores of First Connecticut Lake, caters to the outdoors person seeking adventure. Snowmobilers can ride right from their cabin and buzz over to Canada or Maine through virgin stands of forest on several hundred miles of well-groomed trails. And there are the simple joys of cozying up by your wood fire in your own cabin after a day in the snow.

I've stayed in Pittsburg several times, and it's important that a visitor understand this is a remote area, with few of the conveniences of a North Conway. Don't expect to run out and see a movie, or make a short drive to a restaurant. Pittsburg is not for everybody, but that's the very thing that makes it special to the hardy breed of winter lover. While the wind and the cold can be fierce in this wild region, so too can the rewards: a moose lopping down the side of the road or a salmon coming up through the ice at the end of your line.

The beauty of Northern New Hampshire is that the experiences can range from the comfort of a well-appointed lodge to roughing-it atmosphere of Pittsburg--something for everyone where the snow is measured by the foot not the inch!

Tall Timber Lodge:
talltimber.com
800-835-6343

An Eskimo in New Hampshire
(Pittsburg)

Indian Stream snakes southward through a lush green valley fringed by pointed firs and spruce before its waters join with that of the Connecticut River. Along its bank on Tabor Road is small cemetery with graves of the Civil War Veterans, hardscrabble farmers, and founding founders of the township of Pittsburg, New Hampshire. Although the cemetery is in the far northern tip of the state and just a stone's throw from Canada, it isn't exactly Eskimo country. So why is there a grave of an Eskimo here? To answer that question we need to go back to the year 1897, and follow the tortured life of Minik, a young Eskimo boy from northwestern Greenland.

Minik's voyage from the obscurity of living the normal life of a polar Eskimo to becoming a New York sensation began when he came in contact with famed explorer Robert Perry. During one of Perry's missions to Greenland he met Minik, his father and four other Eskimos, all of which he brought back with him to New York. The Eskimos were presented as specimens to the American Museum of Natural History, and put on display to a paying public. Unfortunately, like Native Americans, the Eskimos had little resistance to strains of influenza, and Minik's father and three others became sick and died. Another was quickly returned to Greenland. That left Minik alone in New York, where he was adopted by the well-to-do Wallace family, and remained a public oddity and "specimen" (while also being studied by anthropologists) for twelve years.

Minik's story becomes even more bizarre when, while visiting the American Museum of Natural History, he discovers the skeleton of his father on display. As one can imagine Minik was outraged and sickened, but the museum considered his father's remains their property and they were not returned to Greenland. To make matters worse, Minik's adoptive family fell on hard times and Minik subsequently tried several times to gain passage on a ship and return to his native Greenland. He was finally successful in 1909, but after twelve years away from home, he felt as out of place there as he did in New York.

Caught between two cultures, Minik decided to return to America in 1916, and it is here that we learn how he came to live in northern New Hampshire. Minik sought employment as a logger and took a train to North Stratford and then proceeded by open wagon to Pittsburg where he joined a mix of French Canadians, Finns, Poles and local Yankees at the lumber company bunkhouse. He worked through the winter chopping trees, clearing brush for slick roads, and generally enjoying life in the woods. For the first time in many years, Minik felt at peace.

When the lumber camps closed in spring, Minik decided to stay on New Hampshire, having become good friends with a local farmer named Afton Hall. Afton invited Minik to live with his family at their small farm high on a hillside just west of Pittsburg Center in Clarksville.

Minik enjoyed the farm work, and fit right in with the Hall family. During his free time he explored the rugged hills and swift-flowing Connecticut River. His life began to settle into a pattern and when autumn came Minik was back at the lumber camp bunkhouse with Afton, ready for another season.

Minik's happiness however did not last long. When the flu swept through the logging camp, Minik was one of the loggers that fell ill. Afton Hall took Minik to his Clarksville home and tried to nurse him back to help, but Minik died, and that is how the Eskimo from Greenland came to be buried in this beautiful spot at the top of New Hampshire.

A fascinating and in-depth look into Minik's life and times can be found in the book, *Give Me My Father's Body*, by Kenn Harper published by Steerforth Press.

The Indian Stream Cemetery can be found just off Route 3 in Pittsburg along the banks of Indian Stream on Tabor Road. Minik's grave is at the rear of the cemetery about half way between either end. (The grave uses Minik's adopted last name of Wallace.) His friend Afton Hall is buried nearby, but toward the side of the cemetery near Tabor Road.

The Hall farmstead was located on a hill overlooking Pittsburg Center and Lake Francis. To reach the site turn off Route 3 onto Route 145 and cross the Connecticut River. Take your first left and then your first right, climbing Crawford Road. The restored white-colored farmhouse is now privately owned and is on your left near the crest of the hill.

Magnetic Hill, Moose and Bear Tree Inn: the Connecticut Lakes Region (Pittsburg)

Pittsburg, New Hampshire enjoys two notable distinctions: it's the northernmost town in the state and the largest. Even more importantly, for the outdoor lover, Pittsburg is among the wildest places in New England, headwaters of the Connecticut River and home of a sizable moose population.

Route 3 is the primary road through the region and exploring the adjacent logging roads and paths almost always leads to adventure. The trout fishing is also first rate, with great angling in the cold, oxygenated waters of the Connecticut River and the series of lakes which the river runs through.

Visitors should travel the entire length of Pittsburg, following Route 3 from south to north. One of the first points of interest is Indian Stream, a beautiful brook flowing southward toward the Connecticut River, which crosses Route 3 at the southern end of Pittsburg. Photography buffs will want to make side trips up the river's east and west sides. On the east side is a road that goes by three handsome barns with matching cupolas, and on the west side is Indian Stream Road, a quiet dirt lane where a sign a mile up the road says it all: "Welcome to Indian Stream Republic -- God's Country."

Back on Route 3 you will soon reach the village of Pittsburg with a covered bridge over the Connecticut, followed by some fine fishing at the tail water below Murphy Dam at the western end of Lake Francis. There are a series of lakes along Route 3 including the four Connecticut Lakes with sprawling First Connecticut Lake being the southernmost and tiny Fourth Connecticut Lake resting on the Canadian border which is the official source of New England's longest river.

After passing Lake Francis there will be a road on the right that leads to Lake Francis State Park with camping and picnicking spots. This road also passes over Perry Stream at an iconic covered bridge.

Another side road off Route 3 leads to Bear Tree Cabins at The Glen, one of the area's premier sporting lodges for those who love a lakeside setting and fantastic food. Located on 180 acres of curving shoreline, it's a special place, a quiet retreat for those who love the North Country, including those interested in a close-to-nature destination wedding. The lodge's large common room with huge stone fireplace is the perfect place for guests to share fishing and moose stories after enjoying a day of exploring. Several log cabins, situated right on the water's edge, provide a private setting for those who just want to kick back and read, nap or listen to the loons.

The stretch of Route 3 that runs between First Connecticut Lake and Third Connecticut Lake is one of the best places to go "moosing" in New England. The moose are seen most frequently at dusk when they come to the swampy areas next to the road where winter salt has filtered into the water which in turn attracts the moose. The most reliable spot is Coon Brook about a mile or two up Route 3 from The Glen.

Hikers will want check out the Road to Mount Magalloway, just north of First Connecticut Lake. (This is an active logging road with a few deep ruts, so you've got to be on the look-out for logging trucks. This back road also crosses the Connecticut River, where it is fly-fishing only/catch and release.) To reach the path to Mount Magalloway follow the signs for the tower and you will arrive at a small parking lot at its end. The hike from the parking area to the tower is 1.1 mile and is steep. (Another side road leads to Scott Bog, a secluded pond nestled in the hills.)

Heading farther north on Route 3 will bring you to the Customs Station at the border with Canada. If you want to see the source of the Connecticut River at Fourth Connecticut Lake, this is where you will park. The trail is about a mile long, but is difficult as it climbs a ridge along the clearing that marks the international border between the two countries.

Rather than end your outing at the border, take the time to cross into Canada and go about a mile to the bottom of Magnetic Hill. Turn the car around (heading back toward the United States), and park at the base of the hill. Then put it in neutral and you will be surprised as it rolls backward, going uphill. Optical illusion, mysterious phenomena, or giant magnets? I'll never tell.

Canada does not have a monopoly on the unusual. The history of Pittsburg is quite colorful. It was once known as the Indian Stream Republic, an independent nation that both Canada and United States claimed as its own. But the people who lived in the Republic liked their freedom, and they ran things the way they saw fit, including using a giant potash kettle as a jail!

A Note on The Balsams Resort

Closed for several years, the Balsams is expected to reopen in 2015 or 2016. Located in Dixville Notch on Route 26, the resort suddenly appears around a bend in the road, majestic and breathtaking, like a castle in the wilderness. It's an extraordinary place, a throwback to yesteryear when America offered diversity in its stores, restaurants and hotels, before the chains made our choices homogeneous, bland, and boring. Maybe it's the magnificent setting in the notch, with towering mountains rising on all sides, or maybe it's the hotel itself, looking like a resort in the Swiss Alps, but we are hoping the Balsams reopens soon. It could be the perfect destination getaway for a lover of wilderness to share a weekend with a lover of civilization. If one partner wants to spend all day hiking or fishing, the other can golf or lounge by the pool and both can do so right here.

In the past the Balsams was a self-contained village, with services such as baby-sitting, church services, a 250 seat theater, beauty shop, and barber-shop. For the sports enthusiast there is golf, tennis, hiking trails, alpine and cross-country skiing in the winter, and mountain biking. But I enjoyed what was right outside my door, a large swimming pool overlooking Lake Gloriette and the towering cliffs of the notch.

Bear Tree at The Glen:
www.atbeartree.com
603-538-9995

THE BERKSHIRES AND HILLTOWNS

The Bardwell's Ferry Bridge, High Ledges and the KenBurn Orchards B&B (Shelburne and Conway)

What does "convenient" mean when you want to get away from it all? I think it means holing up in a place like the KenBurn Orchards B&B off Route 2 in Shelburne, Mass., where you can get away and still have plenty to see and do very close by.

This massive farmhouse and surrounding property has been in the same family for nearly 100 of its 130-or-so years. Set on a hill above Route 2 just a few miles west of Interstate 91, it is surrounded by gnarled apple orchards, rows of future Christmas trees and acres of blueberry bushes. A gorgeous specimen of a maple tree towers over the front of the quintessential New England farmhouse.

A sense of calm settled over us as soon as we arrived. We had spent hours on the road, fleeing a snowstorm to the east, cold temperatures and strong winds all day. Inside our cozy room it was snug and quiet, not even the wind could be heard pushing against the old timbers. There is no television or wifi, so we borrowed some of the Sunday paper from the sitting room downstairs, played a CD from the collection in the room and drew a bubble bath in the giant Jacuzzi tub. Bliss.

In the morning, innkeepers Larry and Susan Flaccus set out a sumptuous breakfast. Because there are only three rooms here, we experienced none of the chain hotel-style buffet lines. Instead, Larry acted the part of butler, bringing us juice and coffee, then setting a succession of amazing, mostly-homemade foods before us: apple, cranberry and nut muffins, fresh bread, applesauce made from their own orchard, sliced strawberries with Grand Marnier whipped cream, and a stunning clafouti (custard pie) with their own blueberries and raspberries baked in. We had to taste it all, and could barely move when it was over.

The maple syrup on the table indicated a theme of the inn: keeping it local. The innkeepers gladly shared information on artists' cooperatives, sources of produce and eggs, even the local source of their ultra-comfy mattresses. The artwork and furniture throughout the inn was carefully chosen and often features local artisans. Susan can tell a story about nearly each of the paintings she has collected, and would be a perfect partner to explore country auctions with, if she could be lured away from her work.

The inn's other guests were a couple of seasoned hikers who shared infor-

mation on places to see in the area, such as High Ledges and the village of Shelburne Falls. Larry and Susan were likewise helpful, but really opened up when discussing the challenges of an agricultural lifestyle in the 21st Century. They've removed 30 acres of the farm's original apple orchards, Susan said, because invasive plants were taking over and they couldn't find anyone to cultivate the trees. Now, native grasses have been planted in their place, creating new habitat for birds and other wildlife. That means summer visitors will surely enjoy the company of butterflies when they come to pick their own blueberries.

"We will do whatever it takes," said Susan. "I promised my father we will not let it be developed."

Larry was a great source of helpful tips for growing blueberries, including which fertilizer to use and how to prune them. He also talked about mowing a field overgrown with goldenrod at dusk one evening when he turned to see something many people search a lifetime for. "It was a mountain lion, it had that distinctive tail," Larry said, drawing a long curve in the air with his finger. "It was looking for mice in what I had cut."

With that image in mind, we pushed back from the table and ventured outside. The blustery winds continued through the morning, cutting short our visit to the inviting gazebo behind the house. We opted instead for a hike through the snow into a gorge on the property, which Susan says may be "the second-deepest in the state." Down in that chasm, the wind couldn't reach us so we enjoyed a tromp through the snow, reading the tracks of animals that had passed through the hemlocks. Sadly, none appeared to be from the mountain lion but we will surely watch for one in the future.

Later, we followed country roads along the property lines of farms and brooks that criss-cross the landscape, enjoying the panorama that changed over each hill and around every corner. We suggest a route south on Zerah Fisk Road, which winds among pastures and woodlands and past at least one brick farmhouse dated 1812. If you take a left at the base of the valley onto Bardwell Road, you'll eventually come to a charming farm with a pigsty right next to the road, where piglets trot around and sows watch visitors warily. Stay to the right at that same turn, remaining on Zerah Fisk Road and the road takes you to the charming Bardwell's Ferry Bridge, painted red, spanning the Deerfield River, connecting Shelburne and Conway. The narrow wrought iron bridge, built in 1882, gets its name from a ferry operated here by Gideon Bardwell and his descendants from 1784 to 1866. This 198 foot long historic lenticular-truss bridge is one of the oldest and longest remaining.

After examining this bridge drive west to Shelburne Falls, a must at any time of year. Known for its Bridge of Flowers, the quaint village is home to many artists and artisans, as well as more cafes than you might believe. We stopped at McCallum's co-op, where you can get any sort of healthful food or drink imaginable. Walking across the bridge, we did some window shopping and ended up at the spot where you can safely look down on glacial potholes in the rock of the Deerfield River, which flows over a dam in the center of town. The rock here is worn smooth from ages of rushing water, causing a bluish tint to show through. Depending on the time of year and water flow, the potholes lend to a watery spectacle of eddies and cascades, its noise pushing the modern world to the background.

It never ceases to amaze us that there are natural wonders like the potholes and the inn's gorge just steps from the built environment. We decided to come back in warmer weather for more hiking, and in the springtime we spent a pleasant morning climbing to the rocky summit of High Ledges in Shelburne. (Directions below) Owned by Massachusetts Audubon, this wildlife sanctuary encompasses over 500 acres of biologically diverse forested hills which include beaver ponds, brooks, stonewalls, birch groves and open fields. Best of all, there are several miles of hiking trails where you are as likely to see a deer or wild turkey as you are another hiker. We were the only visitors, and it was a singularly joyful feeling to have the woods all to ourselves.

When we were able to return for a hike to the Ledges, we began by sauntering along a woodland path shaded by maples, red pines and hemlocks, we first headed toward the overlook, stopping to examine an old stone wall and a giant white oak with gnarled and twisting branches. In the understory, mountain laurel glittered in the sun and a pileated woodpecker swooped by in its distinctive flight, no doubt looking for tree to peck away at in search of insects. A small vernal pool lay on the south side of the path and that too drew our attention. Vernal pools are the breeding places of wood frogs and salamanders, which emerge from the primordial ooze of the pool in the spring. They choose these pools because there are no predator fish in them.

It is only a ten minute walk to the ledges, where an old cottage is tucked away on the rocky promontory. On clear days you can see all the way to Mount Greylock, the tallest peak in Massachusetts. As you stand at the ledge the vista to your left includes the village of Shelburne Falls and Buckland, while to your right are the more isolated hills sloping down to meet the blue-gray waters of Deerfield River, snaking through green foliage. This ledge is the kind of place to bring a blanket, snack, and special friend to relax and drink in the scenery and listen to the murmuring breezes wash up and over the hilltop, which is exactly what we did.

From the ledge you can take long walks either westward to West Beaver Pond or northeastward along North Trail and Lady's Slipper Trail. The hiking can be as short as an hour or as long as four hours depending on how far you wish to explore.

Bicyclists or country road drivers might want to make High Ledges a stop on a loop ride that begins and ends on Route 2. Begin your ride by turning off Route 2 in Shelburne onto Little Mohawk Road, which, is 5.4 miles west of the Greenfield Rotary. Little Mohawk Road will be on your right, and you should be looking for a church steeple and a sign for Davenport Maple Farm and Springbrook Campground. Follow Little Mohawk Road for 1.3 miles, passing some gorgeous country vistas, until you come to Patten Road where you should turn left. Proceed on Patten Road for 1.1 mile to a dirt road on your left that will have a small sign for High Ledges. The parking area is a half-mile down this road.

After exploring High Ledges you can return to Route 2 on different roads that lead through woodlands and past rolling farmland and apple orchards. When you leave High Ledges follow the dirt road back to Patten Road, but this time when you come to Tower Road (in about half a mile) turn right. Follow Tower Road about half a mile then turn left on Cooper Lane Road. Most of Cooper Land Road is a dirt road with very few cars on it, affording you a good chance to see some wildlife, such as coyotes and red fox which hunt the fields for mice. It is only a mile and half back to Route 2.

KenBurn Orchards B&B:
www.kenburnorchards.com
413-625-6116

Directions To High Ledges: •
At the junction of Rt 2 and Rt I-91 continue west on Rt 2 toward Shelburne for 6 miles. Take a right onto Little Mohawk Rd and bear left at the next junction onto Patten Rd. Continuing on Patten Rd, bear left at the next junction and then bear right. The sanctuary entrance is the sec-

ond left at approximately 0.8 miles. A small parking area is located a few hundred yards down the sanctuary road on the left; an overflow parking area is also on the left, just as you turn onto the sanctuary road. Parking areas may be inaccessible from December to May due to snow and mud.

Thoreau, Mount Greylock & The Williams Inn
(Adams, Lanesboro, Williamstown)

On Mothers' Day in 1990, drenching rains pounded Mount Greylock in the Berkshires, causing a massive rock slide on the eastern slope. Trees were uprooted, and a large gash of exposed rock became visible as far away as the center of Adams. With most of the trees and brush gone, the profile of a man's face emerged from the granite. It is an angry face, with a mouth twisted downward, jaw jutting forward, high cheekbones and a bald or shaved head with only a lock of hair hanging behind. Many think it resembles an Indian. Perhaps it is Chief Greylock, come back to reclaim his mountain.

At 3,491 feet, Greylock is the highest peak in Massachusetts. The origin of its name is uncertain. Some believe it was named for the dark grey clouds that shroud or "lock" the mountain in winter. But others say it was named after Chief Greylock, a Mohawk leader who lived northwest of the mountain. Now that I've seen the rock slide and its facial profile, I'm inclined to believe the latter story. I like a little mystery.

The rock slide and profile are best seen from Gould Road in Adams. The profile is not easily discernible at a casual glance. One has to know that the face is pointing to the right as you look at it; then it all becomes clear. Perhaps the chief has come back to express his displeasure over encroaching development near the base of the mountain. Perhaps he is reminding us to care for the earth, our common mother.

On an early Sunday morning I coaxed my ancient Subaru up the 10-mile access road from Lanesboro. First I climbed through a forest of oak, beech, birch and hemlocks. Then, after rounding hairpin turns, the trees in the upper elevation changed to mostly conifers (such as red spruce and balsam fir), clinging to the rocky slopes. Periodic views to the west appeared, adding to the sense of exhilaration I get whenever climbing a mountain – whether by foot or by car. Near the summit the trees were smaller; some stunted and twisted from too much wind and not enough soil. Not long ago, much of the mountain was devoid of trees and the east face suffered serious erosion from continual logging.

As my car coughed and growled, I thought of naturalist and author Henry David Thoreau. Even if there had been automobiles in his day, he never would have driven to the top. My guilt increased when I later learned that not only did he blaze his own trail to the summit, he walked here all the way from his home in Concord. Much has been said about Thoreau, but few acknowledge his remarkable physical stamina.

Thoreau's trek to Greylock came at a time when he was going through deep personal doubts. Just a few weeks earlier, he had accidently burned down a vast tract of forest in his native Concord. Perhaps he came to Greylock for escape and contemplation, knowing instinctively that mountains have therapeutic powers.

As great as his stamina was, his planning (or lack of personal concern) left something to be desired. The summit was so cold that he covered himself with boards to ward off the overnight chill. He wrote: "As it grew colder towards midnight, I at length encased myself completely with boards, managing even to put a board on top of me, with a large stone on it to keep it down, and so slept comfortably." I believe the part about the boards, but I'm not so sure about the comfortable sleep.

When I reached the summit, I forgot my guilt about driving up. Here was a sacred place, a cathedral open to the heavens. The 3,491-foot peak has vistas of up to 100 miles, past the Berkshire Hills into the Green Mountains to the north and the rolling hills of New York to the west. The silence was wonderful, but if you stare out from this vantage point long enough you just might hear echoes from the past – the chants of Chief Greylock or Thoreau's chattering teeth.

I was so impressed with Mount Greylock and the surrounding hills that I came back the following weekend, taking my daughter Kristin with me on our annual father/daughter weekend. We chose Williamstown to explore because I'd never been there. It turned out to be a great choice. Williamstown is so handsome and so tastefully laid out that it ranks right up there on my list of most appealing country towns. Located in the northwest corner of the Berkshires, Williamstown is a small college town, offering the visitor a wide assortment of cultural and outdoor activities.

When we arrived at Williamstown, we took an hour and explored this very walkable town on foot. There were pleasing views in every direction, historic homes, churches, and rolling lawns, all framed by mountains. The campus of Williams College lines the main road, and the college's many stone and brick buildings add grace to the town. The feeling I had while walking was one of spaciousness. You couldn't help but realize the community had pride in every detail of its appearance.

The white man's settlement in Williamstown began in 1750. The town was first known as West Hoosac. A blockhouse, stockade and fort were built at the present site of the Williams Inn as a refuge from repeated attacks during the French and Indian Wars. When peace came to the region in 1760, settlers arrived in droves, clearing the woods for agricultural use. Today, many of the farms are reverting back to forest, but the country feeling has not left.

After exploring the town's center we went to the renowned Sterling and Francine Clark Art Institute. This houses one of the largest collections of Renoir works in the world. My knowledge of French impressionist painters is limited, but you don't need familiarity to feel moved by beauty. Besides the paintings by Renoir and other masters, I was taken with the works of American artists such as Homer, Sargent and Remington.

We left man's creations of beauty to visit nature's driving next to Field Farm, owned by the Trustees of Reservations. This 294-acre country estate lies at the foot of the Taconic Range and is home to wild turkey, coyote, bear, deer and fox. Osprey, wood ducks, kingfishers and herons visit the pond and marshes. There is even a bed and breakfast in a large home that offers sweeping views of the fields, forest and Mount Greylock.

Back in Williamstown we took another short walk, this time along the banks of the Hoosic River (also known as the Hoosac River). Just beyond Williams College is an access road to ball fields. This in turn leads to a wonderful river walk that begins near Eph's Pond in a flood plain area that is one of the lowest elevations in the Berkshires. The woods here have giant cottonwoods, box elder and sycamore (identified by the splashes of white on the grey-brown bark). The river ran swiftly, coursing with rifles over small stones. It appeared to be a great place for trout fishing.

That night we stayed at the Williams Inn, located adjacent to the common in the center of town. This features 100 guestrooms on three stories, all decorated in Colonial style but with modern comforts like an indoor pool. The room in which we stayed was quite comfortable.

Not all trips go according to plan, and sometime during the middle of the night, Kristin awoke with an extremely high fever. The inn's manager came to the rescue, going out to purchase Tylenol so I could stay with Kristin. Now that's the kind of service that brings customers back.

The Williams Inn:
www.williamsinn.com
(413) 458-9371

Mount Greylock State Reservation
(413) 499-4262

Clark Art Institute:
www.clarkart.edu
(413) 458-9545

Field Farm:
www.ttor.org
(413) 458-3144

Supplemental Directions to Hoosic River Trail: Park on Stetson Road across from Eph's Pond, near barrier gate on right. Follow paved lane bordered by light poles to evergreens, and turn right. Follow about 20 feet to trail on left leading into woods. Proceed to river.

Walking the Mahican-Mohawk Trail
(Shelburne)

When people think of the town of Shelburne in the Hilltowns of Massachusetts they usually conjure up images of the village of Shelburne Falls with its Bridge of Flowers and glacial potholes. South of the village, however, along the banks of the Deerfield River, is a walking path called the Mahican-Mohawk Trail, said to follow one of the original routes of the Native American.

The section of trail I've hiked begins at Route 2 just 300 yards east of the police station in Shelburne. There is a pull-out on the south side of the road where a sign says "4.8 miles to Bardwell Ferry." I've walked about three miles of this trail and then retraced my steps back to the parking area. On my next trip I hope to do the whole section, leaving a bike at the Bardwell Ferry Bridge so I can pedal back to my car. Even better would be to go with a friend and leave one car at each end.

From the parking area by the police station the trail passes through tall white pines and plantation of red pines. You soon reach a T-intersection where you should go left, following a ridge above the Deerfield River. There are some spectacular views looking east along the river valley.

As you follow the river downstream to the east you will pass through a nice stand of beech and hemlock after five minutes of hiking. One of the beech trees is especially large and its smooth gray trunk looks like the leg of giant elephant. Here you might want to go off trail and bushwhack up the ridge because there are more live trees.

Shelburne, like most towns along the Deerfield River, has plenty of wildlife, from turkeys to coyotes. Lately the black bear population has been growing, and people and bears are coming in to contact with one another more often. While I have not seen a bear here, I have seen their tracks. Usually the bear hears or smells you long before you even know it's nearby, and the bear either moves off or stays hidden letting you pass. Should you see a bear and it doesn't run off, chances are it has cubs nearby. That's when you want to slowly back off.

Back on the trail, our walk descends down a gradual slope and over a wooden footbridge, passing an enormous oak tree. You will then enter an open field where you should pause and scan the edges looking for deer. Continuing along the river ridge, you will pass under some power lines. Glacial boulders, called erratics because of the way they haphazardly fell off the retreating glaciers, dot the woods. Mountain laurel twinkles in the understory of the forest, and a side trail will take you down to the edge of the river. This is fine to stop for a snack and let the river be your music, before continuing toward Bardwell Ferry. Your walk will take you past a New England Power Company dam and then the path will follow the curve in the river to the east, passing once again beneath power lines. This was the point where I turned back to the parking lot, but according to my map it's just another mile to the Bardwell's Ferry Bridge. (When you reach a railroad bridge, there is no formal trail, but it's just an eighth of a mile along the river until you reach the Bardwell's Ferry Bridge.)

Old Mill Sites and Rivers of Beauty
(Florida, Monroe, Charlemont, West Hawley, Plainfield,
Cummington, and Goshen)

On a warm October morning – a real Indian summer – my brother Mark and I followed the Deerfield River northward, far off the beaten path and into the isolated mountain town of Florida. This is a far cry from the Sunshine State, and not exactly a tourist spot. You won't find Disney World, Busch Gardens or beaches here, but hikers and nature lovers should make it a point to explore this area, as the rewards are many. Especially interesting is the Dunbar Brook Trail, owned by the New England Power Company. That is where Mark I began our morning jaunt.

The trail follows the brook upstream from its confluence with the Deerfield River, climbing into rugged forested hills. Right away I knew I was going to like the place. Instead of the pines and oaks that dominate the area around my home in southeastern Massachusetts, we found massive hemlocks, maples and white birch – as close to the "forest primeval" as I've ever seen. And the brook was a classic mountain stream, surging down the hills, flexing its muscles.

Scenery like this gives your legs their own special energy, and the rhythm of walking was like music. The farther upstream we ventured, the more rugged the land became, with little waterfalls dropping into slick pools below. Beneath the cathedral of trees, ferns grew in the shade – deep green over a blanket of fallen brown leaves. I wondered if Mohawk or Hoosac Indians had once used this same ridge trail.

Just after we crossed a log bridge to the opposite side of the stream, Mark spotted an old millstone in the river. I was surprised to learn that early settlers had lived here, in this wild unforgiving land. But in the 17th and 18th centuries, water-power was a valuable commodity; both grist and lumber mills were erected all along the Commonwealth's rivers and streams.

We didn't find any more evidence of the mill, but five minutes farther up the trail we came upon an old cellar hole. We wondered if this marked the remains of an isolated home, or had there been a little village here that the forest had since swallowed up? It must have been a tough life working this bony land, but to have a home within earshot of the tumbling brook would be wonderful compensation.

Beyond the cellar hole, Dunbar Brook cascades down a series of ledges carved by centuries of falling water, fanning out at the bottom into a wide pool. This is where we finally rested, eating the sandwiches we had packed. The finest restaurant in the state could not duplicate the wonderful taste of those sandwiches; it was the air, the smell of evergreens, and the rigorous walk that made this meal special.

The only recent evidence of man in the area is a hiker's shelter you may find if you venture about an hour up the trail. We crossed Dunbar Brook rather than following the trail where it took a 90 degree turn away from the water and headed straight up-hill. On the other side of the brook we found a few amazing specimens of white pine, one that had to be 15 feet around at its base. Upstream we crossed a footbridge to a high peninsula where Haley Brook empties into Dunbar. On that ridge high above the water was the shelter. If you were hiking with kids and promised to cook lunch over a campfire there, it might be enough to quell the usual complaints about tramping through the woods for an hour (another plus for those with kids: there's a natural cave right on the trail above Dunbar Brook about 45 minutes into the hike, impossible to miss as the trail wraps right around it.) Best way we found out of the shelter area was to retrace our steps, we didn't see a trail through the site.

We lay back on the rocks watching the last of the leaves drop from the beech and maples. When the sun went behind a cloud, the wind kicked up, sending an orange avalanche of leaves tumbling down the hill behind us. Now there was a bite to the air, reminding us of the harsher weather soon to come. We shouldered our knapsacks and headed back downstream.

Although the cool breeze pushed us to return to our car, it occurred to me that returning here in any season would be spectacular. In summer the trail would be fully shaded and cooled by the nearby water. In winter, snowshoeing on such a flat trail with little undergrowth is easy, and in the depths of winter the brook would be a series of frozen cascades, amplifying the bubbling water underneath. The silence of the remote location and the majesty of the forest make it a memorable destination any time.

Back in the car, we passed the dark and forbidding entrance of the Hoosac Tunnel. Completed in 1876, this railroad tunnel took a monumental 25 years to build. It travels four and a half miles straight through the mountain. I could only imagine the conditions the laborers endured during its construction.

It was near the tunnel that we surprised a flock of wild turkeys. Though large birds, they're very quick on foot, and these vanished in the woods. The turkey was Benjamin Franklin's nominee for the United States national bird. If you're only familiar with fat farm turkeys, you might wonder if old Ben was serious. But the wild turkey is a different bird altogether; he's faster, more cautious, and capable of flight.

Later, Mark and I explored some of the town's back roads. One was so steep that we could only climb it in first gear. On the descent, our ears popped as though we were in a jet. We also came across a forlorn cemetery on a wood hilltop. I remarked that perhaps 100 years ago there was a thriving village nearby. "Who knows, maybe in the next 100 years this will be suburbia," Mark said. I shuddered at the thought – we've already seen what development did to the other Florida.

Next, we followed the Deerfield River southward, stopping to fly-fish at a couple of "secret holes." Many anglers regard the Deerfield as Massachusetts' best trout stream, and I have to agree. This was one of the first rivers in the state to have a catch-and-release section, and the experiment has been a success. The result is bigger trout, and more of them.

The stretches of whitewater also attract the attention of experienced canoeists, kayakers, and rafters. And for those who have never run the rapids, there are outfitters – such as Zoar Outdoor and Crab Apple Whitewater – that rent equipment, provide lessons and offer guided excursions on the river.

I try to avoid Route 2, The Mohawk Trail, because the traffic moves too quickly for a slow-poke like me. (Of course, it can get very crowded during October, when the leaf peepers are out). So Mark and I turned on Route 8A, first heading north one-fifth of a mile to see one of the region's more scenic covered bridges. Large log railings line the edge of the road, directing your eye to the weather-worn boards of the Bissell Bridge in Charlemont. There are windows inside; it is possible to look out and see the Mill River passing below. Years ago, a bridge such as this would have been the perfect spot for a young couple to park their wagon for a bit of sparkin'.

Bissell Bridge was built in 1951 at the site of another covered bridge that once carried wagons to a nearby iron mine. When the new bridge was completed, the town of Charlemont held a square dance on it to celebrate the occasion!

There are a number of theories about why so many bridges were covered in the 1800s and the early 1900s. Most of these center on horses, because the bridges were built before the age of the automobile. It is said that horses feared crossing water at a height, and by covering a bridge the horses would get the impression they were simply entering a barn. The bridges also offered protection for horse, driver and wagons of hay during sudden summer downpours. Still another theory has it that the bridges were covered to prevent horses from slipping on the smooth wooden planking during periods of ice and snow.

But the real reason for covering a bridge has nothing to do with horses. Instead, it relates to the structure itself. Wood exposed to the elements decays faster than wood that is protected, and a roof shelters the bridge's important structural members in the span. Periodic replacement of the roof would be far simpler than repairing the timbers below.

Mark and I stopped here, taking pictures and examining the bridge's construction. Visiting a covered bridge can take you back to simpler time. As we sat quietly by the river, I could almost hear the squeak of the wagon wheels and the thud of hoofs on the wooden planks.

Heading south on 8A, we soon passed the wilds of the Savoy and Hawley State Forests. This is an isolated, rugged region, with only a handful of homes and an unmarked church hugging the hillside. The road was most memorable for the rough-legged hawk that flew by with a snake in its talons. We searched the woods for bears, knowing this part of Massachusetts has more black bears than any other.

We also wondered if the "ghost of the forest," the mountain lion, was living nearby. Though these creatures are considered extinct in New England, reports of cougar sightings persist – especially here in the Berkshire Hills and the woods of the Quabbin Reservoir area. On my last visit to the region, I met a man who said he saw a lion cross the Cold River, just a few miles from here. Count me as one of the believers. If there are cougars roaming these forests, it's unclear whether they were illegally released from captivity or are truly wild. It's also uncertain whether or not there is a breeding population. But it's possible; there are certainly enough deer to support them.

We passed through the sleepy village of Plainville and turned onto Central Street, a fine old country road lined by ancient maples, woods and fields.

Then Mark and I stopped to fish a stream on Stage Road, where the water cascades over the remains of an old stone dam at a former mill site. Beaver had made good use of this spot. Their dam of sticks and mud was erected just above the mill site, forming a good-sized pool of water for their protection. From mill pond to beaver pond – I wondered what the former mill owner would have thought.

Two young boys were fishing downstream from us, one of them furiously trying to free his lure from a tree. For a moment I considered going over to give a hand and perhaps offer some casting tips. But then I remembered the last time I gave a couple of youngsters some fishing advice. When I finished telling them about the habits of trout and the best lures to use, one of the boys opened his battered and rusted tackle box to show me something. Crammed inside was a fat brown trout, no less than 16 inches long. I decided to keep my advice to myself.

When we reached Cummington, we followed Route 9 west a couple of miles to West Cummington. Here we stopped and took photos of an old church nestled in the woods. It rises above the village and the river below, like a sentinel guarding this peaceful place.

On past trips to the Cummington-Goshen area I've visited the DAR Forest. This is a great place for swimming and boating. It also has one of the few fire-towers in the state that is open to the public. From the top, there are commanding vistas over the pines and hemlocks that seem to stretch endlessly.

Near the corner of Route 9 and Route 112 South, we stopped at the Creamery Grocery for a drink. Striking up a conversation with one of the locals, I remarked how the dairy farms gave these little towns their special character and open views. But my new friend said the farmers were in trouble, and later research proved him right: Massachusetts has only half the dairy farms it did just 10 years ago. Country life is not always as idyllic as it seems.

From the Creamery Grocery, it's just a couple of miles south on Route 112 to what I consider the perfect home. The 23-room William Cullen Bryant Homestead rests on a hill overlooking rolling countryside and the valley of the Westfield River. A view like this should be enjoyed from a country porch, and this home has a beauty. Maybe that's where the poet and writer Bryant found his peace and inspiration.

This place has an enduring appeal. In 1835, Bryant's widowed mother went into debt and was forced to sell the rambling home. Thirty years later, long after his mother had died, William Cullen Bryant – now a successful poet and newspaper editor – bought it back. Anyone who sees the place will understand why. Cummington could lure anyone back.

Zoar Outdoor:
www.zoaroutdoor.com
800-532-7483

Crab Apple Whitewater:
www.crabapplewhitewater.com
 800-553-7238

Mohawk Trail Association:
www.mohawktrail.com
413-743-8127

The William Cullen Bryant Homestead is owned by The Trustees of Reservations and is open seasonally: 413-532-1631.

The Dunbar Brook Hiking Trail can be reached via River Road near the Florida-Monroe border.

Meadows, Tall Trees, and the Warfield House Inn
(Charlemont)

One of the most enjoyable walks I've taken this year was on the Nature Trail Loop at Mohawk Trail State Forest in Charlemont, Massachusetts. The walk offers a variety of terrain and natural features, including meadows, towering white pines, a rushing river, and habitat that is home to bears, wild turkeys, white-tailed deer and bobcat.

Mohawk Trail State Forest is located along Route 2 in Charlemont, and encompasses hundreds of acres in both the river valley and the mountains. When you visit the forest stop in at the Ranger station and see if they have any trail maps available. If they are out of maps don't worry; the Nature Trail is easy to follow and is a wonderful introduction to the park. From the ranger station follow the roadway to the Group Camping area, and then walk down a dirt road that is blocked by a gate. About a quarter mile down the dirt road you will see a sign on your left for the start of the Nature Trail. Follow the path beneath the white pines, heading in a northeast direction. A stone wall borders the trail on the left. If you look carefully you will see that on the right side of the stonewall the trees are relatively small indicating this was where the pasture was, but on the left side the trees are huge suggesting that area has not been logged or cleared for perhaps two hundred years.

On my last hike it had rained just prior to my arrival and the understory of mountain laurel glistened. The woods were cool and fresh, and when the sun broke out I almost expected to hear a symphony, such was its beauty. In the distance there was music of sorts; the rushing waters of the Deerfield River, one of Massachusetts top trout streams. Another sound reached my ears as well, this one the distant drumming of a ruffed grouse.

After walking ten minutes you will arrive at a broad meadow. Before entering, stop at the edge of the woods and scan the grassy fields to see if there is any wildlife moving about. Often you must stand still for five or ten minutes until your eyes pick out a shape or shadow on the other side of the field. On my way in I saw a raven perched on a trail sign at the center of the meadow, and later, when I left the area, two wild turkey cautiously emerged from the woods and into the sunlight on the east side of the meadow. Even if no wildlife is present the meadow is a treat; it's like walking through the bottom of a bowl, surrounded by forested hills.

The trail cuts through the meadow heading to the north, skirting the lofty heights of Todd Mountain. Near the end of the field a sign points to the right for the Nature Trail, but you should follow the path straight into the woods to see some enormous trees and rocky crags. The path is narrow as it leads along a ridge with Todd Mountain to your left and the lowlands of the Deerfield River to the right. Bright green moss and ferns give the woods an enchanting look and there are glacial erratic boulders scattered about. As I hiked this rugged hillside I felt my primitive self emerge, aware that I was walking quietly, looking from side to side and living in the moment. In retrospect it seemed like a call from our ancestors, the hunter-gathers who probably walked like this every day of their lives.

In two spots along the trail the granite ledges form a kind of shelter, and a real cave lies to the west just 400 feet from the trail. (There is no trail to the cave so it may take some careful searching and pay attention to where you are going so you don't get lost.) The main trail was once part of the Mahican-Mohawk Trail and is marked with green discs nailed to trees. Some of the larger tree species you will see along the trail include hemlock, ash, and maple. This trail continues for some distance, but after 15 minutes of walking through the woods I retraced my steps back to the meadow.

Once in the meadow, follow the signs toward the Deerfield River, continuing on the Nature Trail. The trail follows a 200-year-old cart-path and begins to angle back toward the dirt road you started your hike on. You will pass a vernal pool on the left followed by a second meadow, called the Lower Meadow, which has two apple trees growing in its center.

Follow the trail closer to the Deerfield River toward the southern end of the Lower Meadow where large sugar maples grow. The view looking back north makes a fine shot for photographers. This would be a great spot for a cabin, and in fact, just a few feet up the trail is a marker indicating the Wheeler Family homestead once stood here. Next, the trail widens and curls away from the river bringing you back to the dirt road that will lead you to your car. You might want to stop and check out the Trees of Peace, a huge grove of white pines. From the dirt road about 300 feet east of the gate look for a strip of orange tape hanging from a tree opposite a large boulder. A small trail will lead you to the trees where a sign explains that the white pines were considered trees of peace by many Native American tribes. Towering over 150 feet the trees are among the tallest in New England and are named after two Mohawk leaders, the Jake Swamp Tree and the Joe Norton Tree.

In total the walk took me about two hours with plenty of stops. For a return trip, take the trail to the summit of Todd Mountain, for an awe-inspiring view at Indian Lookout. Legend has it that the Native Americans used this vantage point in the 1700's to keep tabs on the advancing settlements of the colonists. Native American experts have also explained that the summit trail was used by natives, when they needed to move quickly – running 40 miles in a day was not uncommon if there was an urgent reason. The hike to the top takes between one and two hours, and in some places mountain laurel crowds the trail making visibility difficult. This section of the Berkshires is like the Continental Divide: the Cold River and Deerfield Rivers below the mountain feed into the Connecticut River flowing through New England, while all the rivers to the west of these hills flow toward New York.

At the summit, hikers will notice that the trees on the south facing side of the mountain are much smaller than on the north side. Fire raced up the south side of the mountain approximately 140 years ago, but the flames were stopped by wind or moisture when they reached the ridge near the summit. Thus the oldest trees are on the north side. Deeply furrowed bark covered with lichen, some of the trees look like large bonsai, while others tower overhead.

People might expect the oldest trees to be the largest, but because of the rocky soil, wind and high elevation, they are not the tallest in the park. That honor goes to the giants farther down the north side of the mountain, below the 1,100 foot elevation. Many years ago I hiked here with old growth tree expert Bob Leverett, who pointed out stands of hemlock, white pines, black birch, and red oak that stretched to the sky, making the heart sing. A couple trees dated back all the way to the late 1500's. I asked him how much bigger the trees would get, and he said "not much. Trees, like people, get most of their growth early. They'll exhibit 'middle-age spread,' but they may live to 300 years of age without getting much taller." I remember Leverett pointing to a large pine far up the ridge where it was framed by the sky. "Notice how the really large pines have branches that are so heavy they begin to pull downward, whereas the younger trees branches are on a small incline."

With each step Bob and I began to see more of the individual trees and less of the forest, even noticing a buck scrape on a small sapling. And farther along was a buck rub on the forest floor where the buck had raked back all the leaf litter, marking its territory with acrid-smelling urine, warning other bucks to stay away during the rut or mating season. In the fall, bucks have one thing on their mind: reproduction. A deer's behavior transforms from shy and elusive to bold and aggressive. Males will battle over females, locking antlers in fight. Hunters have told of seeing one buck flip another with its antlers, or coming across two dead bucks, antlers intertwined. The deer had died when the antlers could not become extricated and both died of starvation.

Nature can be cruel, but the tall trees of Mohawk State Forest show us a grandeur that will make you return again and again.

For overnight lodging you can't beat the Warfield House Inn, in nearby Charlemont. Situated high on a hilltop overlooking the Deerfield River Valley, the views from the inn rival those at High Ledges. Lodging at the Warfield House Inn includes a full homemade breakfast, handsome country rooms, a hot tub on the porch, and a restaurant and pub that is open year round in the late afternoon and evening. On weekends the restaurant is open for breakfast from 8-10am. The inn encompasses five hundred acres and there are some great walks to take through the meadows. Children will love the horses, llamas, emus, and chickens-- adventurous kids can even go out to the chicken coop and get their own eggs for breakfast!

The Warfield House Inn:
www.warfieldhouseinn.com;
888-339-VIEW

Sugar Maples and Waterfalls
(Chesterfield, Worthington, Middlefield & Chester)

I love traveling with a river by my side, so I turned off Route 143 and followed the Westfield River southward. Just beyond the crossroads at the village of Chesterfield is a canyon carved by the rushing waters of Westfield River's west branch at Chesterfield Gorge. Towering above the river are sheer granite cliffs; down below are smooth, water-worn rock formations that look something like waves. The waters pound through the narrow passage in spring while the summer's low water is the picture of tranquility.

At the upper end of the gorge is the stone foundation of High Bridge, which dates to 1739. The bridge was once part of the Boston to Albany Post Road. In the Trustees of Reservations' brochure, I read that, during the Revolutionary War, the Redcoats marched over this bridge heading toward Boston and their ships after being defeated at Saratoga. Try as I might, I simply cannot visualize an army of Redcoats marching through this quiet, forested spot.

After stopping at the Knightsville Dam – where the broad flood plain was shrouded in mist – I went on to Worthington. For me, the rain was a nuisance. But inside the Corners Grocery I heard a very different perspective. A woman with a big smile on her face raised both arms to the sky and said, "Ah, sweet rain, I can almost see the corn dancing." If you make our livelihood off the land, sudden showers can be quite welcome.

Worthington is a good place to visit, no matter the season. Winter brings cross-country skiers while early spring is maple sugar time. Summer is the best season for both hiking and fishing, and fall is perfect for cruising back roads and soaking up the wonderful foliage. When we think of autumn's colors, many of us think of Vermont and New Hampshire, but the Berkshires are equally impressive. The country roads that wind through Worthington are lined by giant sugar maples that can turn a whole hillside bright yellow and orange come October. There are some particularly impressive maples along Route 143 near the Worthington Inn, a handsome colonial farmhouse dating back to 1780. The inn has three guestrooms, five fireplaces and is filled with period antiques. Across the way is a large field where horses graze behind the stone wall.

From Worthington, Glendale Falls is only about five miles as the crow flies. Because of the large tract of forest along the middle branch of the Westfield River, the drive there is more than twice as long. But if you're in the area and you love waterfalls as I do, you won't want to miss it. Cascading 150 feet over rock ledges, Glendale Brook tumbles toward the river valley below. A small footpath follows the brook down the hill, offering a variety of interesting photographic opportunities. I'm partial to the picture at the very top of the falls looking downstream, where the brook suddenly drops from sight.

Surrounding the falls is a forest of hemlock and beech, with an understory of mountain laurel. The serenity there was wonderful. It's easy to take silence for granted, but think how rare it's becoming. Seems there is always noise — cars, TV, radio, even the annoying beep of E-mail on your computer. But, as I walked the woods at Glendale Falls, the only sounds were an occasional bird song and the muted splashing of the brook in the distance. Thank God for quiet places.

Later, with maps spread before me in the parking area of Glendale Falls, I noticed that River Road hugged the middle branch of the Westfield River for a good distance. I decided to take that road, and worry about where it led later.

It was a beautiful drive, an isolated stretch of asphalt with plenty of spots along the river where you could stop to read, write, or just cool your feet. I tried to do all three, but the lure of the trout was too much.

Donning an old pair of sneakers, I walked up the river. The summer's drought made walking easy but catching trout difficult. There was, however, one advantage to low water: when I cast my fly into a tree on the opposite bank, it was relatively easy to wade across and retrieve it. Not the sort of thing to brag about but, if you're in the habit of losing flies, it's nice to be able to save one now and then.

It was hot, so I found a pool deep enough to sit in. With my clothes on the bank, I took special care to place my glasses squarely on top of them. It was only a couple of months earlier that I had a bad experience doing precisely the same thing. At that time, I'd walked a couple miles through the woods, blazing my own trail to reach a river (visions of giant trout make us do crazy things). Later, I went for a swim in the river and when I came out I couldn't find my glasses. Now, only those who wear glasses can understand the panic that swept through me. The thought of trying to negotiate my way out of dense woods with blurry vision was not a prospect I relished. There was a real chance of getting lost or injuring myself. I searched everywhere for the glasses, believing I had placed them atop my clothes. I don't know what I would have done if the sun had not reflected off the metal frames, because the glasses were not on my clothes but on a rock a few feet away in the river. To this day I don't remember putting them there, but I do recall the relief of being able to see again.

This time, the glasses were right where I left them. I let the sun dry me off then found my way back to the car and headed south. The trip was somewhat unusual because I had no real destination in mind. I'd let the road and curiosity be my guide. In his book, Blue Highways, William Least Heat Moon used the same approach to exploration. He wrote, "Had I gone looking for some particular place, rather than any place, I never would have found this spring under the sycamores."

On my map I saw Chester Center. The word "center" often means the old part of town, and this was no exception. An old church, even older homes, and a graveyard were all that made up this forgotten and peaceful place. Later, on Route 8, I chuckled when I saw one of those "Adopt a Highway" signs emblazoned with the name of a Boy Scout troop. Looked to me like the state had gotten the Boy Scouts to become "litter-picker-uppers." Let's hope the Scouts still learn a little woodcraft, like making a fire in the rain.

Worthington Inn:
www.hidden-hills.com/worthingtoninn/
413-238-4441
Chesterfield Gorge is located on River Road in West Chesterfield; swimming is not allowed.
For information, call
413-684-0148.
Glendale Falls is on Clark Wright Road in Middlefield.
For information on The Trustees Naumkeag property,
call 413-298-3239
or see www.ttor.org.

Southern Berkshires in the Slow Lane
(Tyringham, Monterey & New Marlborough)

The back roads above Tyringham took me up the ridge and past the old Shaker homes, plain yet handsome in their simplicity. It was a beautiful hilltop high above the valley, a place where road names retained their original meaning. Meadow Road wound through a golden hayfield, Forest Road passed dark and mysterious woods, and Tyringham Road went through town.

Now I was on Breakneck Road, dropping down the precipitous slope, the ancient Subaru growling in low gear. We churned across green lowlands, over a stream, and through lush pasture before turning onto a main road (actually named Main Road) toward town.

Ahead sat a structural oddity that made me slam on the brakes: a real honest-to-goodness gingerbread house, or so it seemed. Its roof was full of waves and curves in colored patterns of grey, brown and rust, like a marbled stone one finds in a streambed.

Called Santarella, the building has a rich history. Now a special events venue, it was for decades the Tyringham Gallery, owned by Ann Marie and Donald Davis who bought the building in 1947, just after the death of its original owner and designer, Sir Henry Kitson. Kitson was a British-born sculptor whose work (ironically) includes the iconic Lexington Minute Man statue on Battle Road, the cloaked Roger Conant statue in Salem and the Pilgrim Maiden statue in Plymouth as well as many in Vicksburg National Military Park.

The roof of Santarella was fashioned with a rolling effect that recalls the Berkshire hills. English workers were imported for the construction; they labored on this project for more than two years. The roof – which has a thatched look – is made from traditional materials and has an estimated weight of 80 tons.

But the gingerbread house is much more than an amazing architectural feat. Walking through the property on the garden path, one can appreciate the monumental effort that went into creating something different, something special.

The word "Tyringham" has a nice ring to it, and the center of town did not disappoint me. It reminded me of a Vermont village: a low-lying valley of farmland surrounded by green hills. At the center of town I turned off the main road and onto Church Road, which leads to a hillside cemetery behind

Union Church. The view was wonderful. A town such as this ranks high on my list, especially when its backside is as good as its front.

While heading toward the trails at the Cobble, I came across four hikers sitting by the side of the road with their gear spread out around them. There were three boys and one girl, all college-age and all spending the summer hiking the Appalachian Trail (runs through the Cobble). The foursome had started out at Harpers Ferry, West Virginia above five weeks earlier. They had since covered over 500 miles, with the previous night being one of the roughest yet. They said they could find no water supply and were getting desperate when the sky opened in a downpour. Using ponchos, they were able to funnel rainwater into their cooking pot. It seemed like their troubles were over. But as evening turned to night, thunder and lightning came, whipping the trees above. The group spent some tense moments inside their tents, wondering if a tree would come crashing down upon them in the dark.

Most of their journey had been filled with pleasant moments. They especially enjoyed meeting friendly people in small towns along the way. "When we go into town," one of them said, "they can smell us coming and know where we've been! Grooming conditions on the trail are not exactly the best. We have had many folks cook us dinners, and have slept in churches, a monastery, private homes, and barns – a nice change from lean-tos."

Wildlife was varied on the trek; they'd spotted a black bear, wild turkey, even a rattlesnake. "This trip is something we have dreamed of for years, and we plan on going all the way to Mount Katahdin," one of them remarked. All I could say was, "Go for it, before the chains of the working world get you." Such an adventure will provide life-long memories.

And so I left my new friends and ascended the Cobble alone. As I hiked, I imagined this was the start of my journey to Katahdin. What would it be like to be outdoors for weeks, to have no other cares than the path in front of you? Life reduced to its most basic and elemental living. Someday…

The walk up the Cobble is a gentle one, passing through pasture, then woods, and later into a field with goldenrod waving yellow in the breeze. Monarch butterflies floated off in front of me and I felt my spirits soar with them. I was glad I was here alone, free to stop and feel the peace of this place. I lay back, letting my face soak up the September sun.

While in the field I saw two handsome birds. First, a blue bird winged by, and I thought of Thoreau's description, "They carry the sky on their back." Then I spotted a kestrel on a cedar tree. It stayed at the top of the tree, apparently surveying the field for insects or mice. I had a good long look through binoculars at this small falcon, with its rusty back and bluish wings. It is said that kestrels rarely go for larger prey preferring inspects instead. But I once saw one swoop down on a blackbird that was feeding on the ground and kill it in a spray of feathers.

Later I resumed my walk, passing an enchanting stand of white birch and then cresting the summit. Far below, an idyllic Tyringham lay nestled in the valley. When a cloud passed over the sun, it was as though someone had drawn a curtain on the town. Then, just as quickly, the light returned to illuminate the church, the green hills and golden fields. I'm sure there are all types of people living in this valley – both good and bad – but from this vantage point, the town seemed far removed from the troubles that plague the rest of the world.

They say that the Cobble was broken off from nearby Backbone Mountain and flipped over, because the oldest rocks are on the top of the hill. But try as I might, I could not picture the event. The hill seemed too permanent, like God put it here. But perhaps God, like man, changes things after a second look.

The rocks at the Cobble are known as "Tyringham gneiss." Once subjected to great heat and pressure, they have a marbled quality to them, and there are many veins of white quartz mixed with the gneiss. On the trail to the top, you can't miss a tall rock formation standing on its end. This boulder – actually a glacial erratic that was carried here by the ice sheet – seems so out of place that one would think it landed here from outer space.

From the Cobble, I drove south into Monterey, then hit the brakes when I saw River Road. A little way down the road was a small waterfall and broad pools. Here, two boys were swinging out over the grey-green water on a rope, and then dropping with a mighty splash. "What the heck?" I thought, putting on a pair of shorts. Shock is probably not the right word for the feeling that occurred when I hit the water. The cold took most of the air out of my lungs, but I still managed a scream as I motored furiously to shore. Yet, within minutes, I was on the rope again. It was as though years had fallen away; I was 10 years old again, invigorated and totally alive.

River Road led down to New Marlborough, where the village green on Route 57 is a classic, complete with an inn. The Old Inn On The Green was built in 1760 and was an important resting spot for weary travelers making the overland journey from Westfield to Sheffield. The inn also served as a post office in 1806, with mail arriving once a week by horseback. Later, a stagecoach brought the mail daily on the "Red Bird Line." The latter ran from Albany to Hartford one day, and then reversed direction the next.

The inn and common look much as they did long ago, and a tired traveler can still find lodging and dining in this handsome building. For some, the location may be too quiet and out of the way, but for others, that's the very reason to come. One of the best things about the setting is the old Monterey-New Marlborough Road, which begins by the side of the inn and passes northward through woods and fields free of power lines and development. Old stone walls built by settlers more than a century and a half ago still stand firmly along the trail. Farmers built the walls from rocks turned up by the plow, using them to mark their property lines or enclose their herds and flocks. Neighbors helped one another when the job was large. "Stone-bees" were held, with oxen and many strong arms removing the rocks and crafting the walls.

Southfield Road leaves the green and winds toward the Old Buggy Whip Factory, which now houses antique dealers, craft shops and a café. At the nearby village of Mill River, I stopped at the old general store and struck up a conversation with the owner. I remarked how this is my kind of country. He responded by saying, "Yes, it's the last place." He meant that this was one region yet to be developed on a large scale. It really was one of the last best places. To underscore what he said, I went down to Umpachene Falls, where two rivers converge. One of the rivers cascades down a series of ledges before mingling with the other river. A kingfisher, with its distinctive crested head, flew over the river with irregular wing beats. Aside from the bird, I had the place to myself.

The falls are named after a Mahican Indian sachem, and surely Native Americans would have had a village or a camp here. The location would have provided both drinking water and fishing. Indeed, the spot where the rivers join would have been deep enough to float the dugout canoes used by tribes in southern New England. I wondered if these Indians could possibly have foreseen that this would be the "last best place?"

The Old Inn On The Green:
www.oldinn.com
413-229-7924

Along the Housatonic
(Stockbridge, Great Barrington, Egremont, Mount Washington & Ashley Falls)

"What an appealing start to a walk," I thought, surveying the narrow footbridge over the Housatonic. With no traffic to worry about on the other side of the river, off I went over the bridge, then up the trail into the Ice Glen.

The ravine known as the Ice Glen was named for the cool mini-climate within this boulder-filled chasm. Even in late spring, the air is dank and cold, and deposits of ice still linger. Little sunlight enters the bottom of the ravine, and its narrowness and depth help keep temperatures from rising. Above the ravine is a trail that leads to Lara's Lookout, offering exceptional views of Stockbridge and the surrounding countryside. The trail that leads to this hilltop is reached by going left at the fork in the path, just minutes after crossing the suspension bridge. It's only about three-quarters of a mile to the top and the ascent is gradual.

As remarkable as the geology of the Ice Glen is, the real reason I came was for the trees. Bob Leverett, an expert on old-growth forests, first told me about this wonderful place. He described magnificent white pines and hemlocks that have grown here for centuries. Large trees have always fascinated me, and I share Robert Frost's sentiments when he wrote, "If I tire of trees, I seek again mankind."

It would be hard to tire of the trees at the Ice Glen. Some are so large that when you look up, they seem to touch the clouds (making you dizzy in the process). The combination of grand old trees and sheer silence gives the place a mystical, cathedral-like quality.

I was so taken with the giant pines that I wrote to Leverett for more information. He told me that the Ice Glen stand includes two incredibly tall pine trees that are over 140 feet in height, with girths of nine feet. Their age is estimated at 100-150 years. In addition, there is also an old-growth section of trees 300 years old. One exceeds 12 feet in circumference and is 134 feet high. There is also a stand of native red pines. A rare treat indeed and, at 200 years old, probably the oldest in the state.

To fully appreciate the need to preserve the old-growth forest, one must look at man's impact on New England's landscape over the past 400 years. When the first Europeans arrived in the New World, only a tiny portion of land had been cleared by the native Algonkin Indian tribes. Miles and miles of virgin forest served as a home to wolves, bears, and even mountain lions. However, in his quest for more agricultural land and lumber, the white man quickly changed the face of New England. By 1900, 75 to 85 percent of southern New England was either field or pasture. And in northern New England, almost every acre had been logged.

In his beautifully written *Guide to New England's Landscape*, Neil Jorgensen wrote, "In the 19th Century, naturalists were warning New Englanders that fearful consequences would ensue if the countryside became disrobed of trees." That gives us some indication of just how devoid of trees the region was at that time.

Today, much of the land has returned to forest as farmland has been abandoned. But most of the more visible woodlands are comprised of trees under 100 years old. The few remaining old growth tracts are located in hilly regions that were too steep for 19th Century logging techniques.

Finding a patch of forest that has never been disturbed takes the patience, know-how, and physical endurance of men like Leverett. He explained that 400 years seems to be the maximum age a tree can live in this region, although he still has hopes of finding a 500-year old specimen. Besides counting the rings on downed trees, Leverett looks for other clues: no sign of human disturbance, a thriving community of shade-tolerant ferns and herbaceous plants on the forest floor, and seedlings on the ground that are the same species as the adults.

The eastern old-growth tracts do not have the stunning proportions of the Pacific Northwest forests, and it takes a trained eye to spot our remaining patches of ancient woodlands. Leverett's son Bob Jr., who works with his father in searching and cataloguing the virgin stands, said, "The old-growth forest canopy has an unmistakable look – even from three or four miles away."

Another reason I love this region is that there is one fascinating place to explore after another, some within a stone's throw of each other. Monument Mountain, rising 1,700 feet above sea level, is just south of the Ice Glen on Route 7. It has spectacular views, a number of hiking trails, and a rich diversity of flora and fauna. On my visit, I took a moment at the base of the mountain to study the trail signs. On the left was the "easy" trail, and on the right, the "steep" trail. I went right, ignoring the fact that my belt was on its last notch. (The minute you start taking the easy way, the battle of the waistline is lost – or so my theory goes.) The start of the trail was deceptively flat, passing beneath a canopy of maple, ash and beech.

But soon the trail became steeper, and boulders made the footing more difficult. In no time, I was winded. I sat in the shade of some old maples to catch my breath. A couple of hikers passed me – which I didn't mind – but then came a man carrying a two-year-old in a "baby pack." That got me back on my feet. Within half an hour I was on the ridge, where stunted pine, mountain laurel and white birch grew in the sun. I was greeted by a 360 view; the open summit looked like a wonderful place to picnic. That's exactly what Herman Melville, Oliver Wendell Holmes and Nathaniel Hawthorne did when they climbed to the peak in 1850. From that very first meeting, Hawthorne and Melville were life-long friends. (Later, Melville even dedicated Moby Dick to Hawthorne.)

I, too, made friends at the top – a couple who lived nearby. We discussed the differences between western and eastern Massachusetts. I've lived half my life in each part of the state and have observed that while many easterners dream of going west, no one from the Berkshires wants to go east. Residents of western Massachusetts think that the politicians in Boston ignore their part of the state, and many distrust the government. Who can blame them – just read the history of Shays' Rebellion, or the seizure of the Swift River Valley to create Quabbin Reservoir.

One of my favorite villages, South Egremont, is located just south of Monument Mountain on Route 41. The entire downtown area is a National Historic District. The Gaslight Store will make you feel as though you stepped back into the last century, and you can still purchase penny candy for a penny. Nearby is Mom's Country Café, where breakfast is served all day.

My daughter Kristin and I once spent a wonderful father/daughter weekend at the Egremont Village Inn in South Egremont. It was a charming place, an elegant farm and coach house situated on 10 acres of land. Thinking back, I remember how much closer that trip brought the two of us – perhaps the adventure of the journey allowed me to see the child in a new light. On that trip, Kristin seemed almost grown up, a real traveling companion. She responded by treating me as both father and friend.

One of the places we explored was Bash Bish Falls, just down the road in Mount Washington. I've been told the easiest way to reach the falls is via Copake, New York, but we felt adventurous and took the rutted back roads through Mount Washington. I'm glad we did. On the way, five deer bounded out across the road, "flags" waving, and down a steep hillside. One seemed to literally sail over a cliff in the most graceful leap imaginable. Nearby, at a turn in the road, we walked to a rock promenade that offered a spectacular view west to New York.

The falls are probably the most impressive in the Bay State. They drop 200 feet in a series of cascades through granite outcroppings, with the final 80-foot drop divided into two cataracts. There is a trail leading to the top of the falls, where the sound of rushing water combined with the extreme height makes for an exciting walk.

Timber rattlers still inhabit this remote section of the state. They can sometimes be seen sunning themselves in the gorge. Once back on the road, be sure to follow Route 7 south into Sheffield. On the right side are three homes tightly clustered together that date to the 18th and 19th centuries and one now house the town's historic society. In the morning, the sun strikes these handsome structures, making for a wonderful picture.

At Ashley Falls there is a great view of the Housatonic at Bartholomew's Cobble. The Mahican Indians gave the river its name – which means "place beyond the mountains" – while the early settlers called it "Great River." In his book, The Housatonic, Chard Power Smith wrote, "In volume it is of the second order, smaller than the Connecticut 40 miles to the east, or the Hudson 40 miles to the west. Yet it is large enough to suggest the power and majesty of the cosmos, and the first colonists of its banks, men who had seen bigger streams, called it the Great River."

There are numerous bends and marshes on this river, which serves as a migratory stopover for many birds and ducks. Indeed the Housatonic is said to be on the most biologically diverse rivers in the state because of the abundant marble and limestone outcrops that neutralize the acidity of the soil over which it flows. This marble – which dates back 500 million years – can be seen at Bartholomew's Cobble. Many rare and unusual lime-loving plants can also be found here. In April, the flowers of the round-leaved hepatica plant show a range of hues, from pure white to deep cobalt. Along with the hepatica, there are over 450 other species of wildflowers growing here.

One could spend a whole day at the Cobble, first visiting the small natural history museum, then walking the riverside trails. Serious walkers should cross Weatogue Road and follow the paths that pass meadows and head northward to the historic Colonel John Ashley House. Built in 1735, the Colonel Ashley House contains furniture and household objects from the 18th and early 19th centuries. Besides being the oldest dwelling in Berkshire County, it was also the site of the Sheffield Declaration, a petition against British tyranny, written in 1773.

Colonel John Ashley House & Bartholomew's Cobble:
www.ttor.org
413-229-8600

Egremont Village Inn:
www.theegremontvillageinn.com
413-528-9580

Happy Trails!

Invite us to speak to your group

The authors give narrated slide presentations based on Inns and Adventures, and Michael also has presentations for his other books. You can purchase autographed copies, see upcoming presentation schedules, and view dramatic videos at www.michaeltougias.com.

Organizations interested in having Alison or Michael speak can contact Alison at alison.3.oleary@gmail.com

Also by Michael J. Tougias

Rescue of the Bounty: A True Story of Disaster and Survival in Super-storm Sandy (co-author Douglas Campbell)

The Cringe Chronicles: A True and Mortifying Memoir of an Awkward Teen Journey (co-author Kristin Tougias)

A Storm Too Soon: A True Story of Disaster, Survival and an Incredible Rescue

Overboard! A True Blue-Water Odyssey of Disaster and Survival

Fatal Forecast: An Incredible True Story of Disaster and Survival at Sea

Ten Hours Until Dawn: The True Story of Heroism and Tragedy Aboard the Can Do

The Finest Hours: The True Story of the U.S. Coast Guard's Most Daring Sea Rescue (co-author Casey Sherman)

Until I Have No Country: A Novel of King Philip's Indian War

King Philip's War: The History and Legacy of America's Forgotten Conflict (co-author Eric Schultz)

Quabbin: A History and Explorers Guide
The Blizzard of '78

River Days: Exploring the Connecticut River from Source to Sea

Exploring the Hidden Charles

There's A Porcupine In My Outhouse: The Vermont Misadventures of a Mountain Man Wannabe

AMC's Best Day Hikes Near Boston (co-author John Burk)

Derek's Gift: A True Story of Love, Courage, and Lessons Learned (co-author Buck Harris)

Summary of Michael J. Tougias' Latest Books

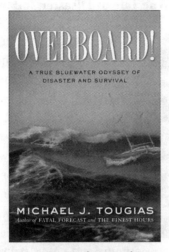

Overboard!
A True Bluewater Odyssey of Disaster and Survival

In early May of 2005 Captain Tom Tighe and first mate Loch Reidy of the sailboat Almeisan welcomed three new crew members for a five-day voyage from Connecticut to Bermuda. While Tighe and Reidy had made the journey countless times, the rest of the crew wanted to learn about offshore sailing—and looking for adventure. Four days into their voyage, they got one—but nothing that they had expected or had any training to handle. A massive storm struck, sweeping Tighe and Reidy from the boat. The remaining crew members somehow managed to stay aboard the vessel as it was torn apart by wind and water. *Overboard!* follows the simultaneous desperate struggles of boat passengers and the captain and first mate fighting for their lives in the sea. (An interview with the author and survivors, along with actual footage from the storm can be found on Youtube Michael Tougias – Overboard Part I, II, III)

"A heart-pounding account of the storm that tore apart a forty-five-foot sailboat. Author Michael Tougias is the master of the weather-related disaster book." – **The Boston Globe**

"Overboard is a beautiful story deserving of a good cry." – **Gatehouse News Service**

"Tougias has a knack for weaving thoroughly absorbing stories – adventure fans need this one!" -- **Booklist**

Fatal Forecast
An Incredible True Tale of Disaster and Survival at Sea

On a cold November day in 1980, two fishing vessels, the Fair Wind and the Sea Fever, set out from Cape Cod to catch offshore lobsters at Georges Bank. The National Weather Service had forecast typical fall weather in the area for the next three days—even though the organization knew that its only weather buoy at Georges Bank was malfunctioning. Soon after the boats reached the fishing ground, they were hit with hurricane-force winds and massive, sixty-foot waves that battered the boats for hours. The captains and crews struggled heroically to keep their vessels afloat in the unrelenting storm. One monstrous wave of ninety- to one-hundred feet soon capsized the Fair Wind, trapping the crew inside. Meanwhile, on the Sea Fever, Captain Peter Brown (whose father owned the Andrea Gail of *The Perfect Storm* fame) did his best to ride out the storm, but a giant wave blew out one side of the pilothouse, sending a crewmember into the churning ocean. Meticulously researched and vividly told, Fatal Forecast is first and foremost a tale of miraculous survival. Most amazing is the story of Ernie Hazard, who had managed to crawl inside a tiny inflatable life raft— only to be repeatedly thrown into the ocean as he fought to endure more than fifty hours adrift in the storm-tossed seas. By turns tragic, thrilling, and inspiring, Ernie's story deserves a place among the greatest survival tales ever told. As gripping and harrowing as *The Perfect Storm*—but with a miracle ending—Fatal Forecast is an unforgettable true story about the collision of two spectacular forces: the brutality of nature and the human will to survive.

"Tougias skillfully submerges us in this storm and spins a marvelous and terrifying yarn. He makes us fight alongside Ernie Hazard and cheer as he is saved . . . a breathtaking book." —**Los Angeles Times**

"Ernie Hazard's experiences, as related by Tougias, deserve a place as a classic of sea survival history."—**The Boston Globe**

"Tougias spins a dramatic saga. . . . (He) has written eighteen books and this is among his most gripping." —**National Geographic Adventure Magazine**

Ten Hours Until Dawn
The True Story of Heroism and Tragedy Aboard the Can Do

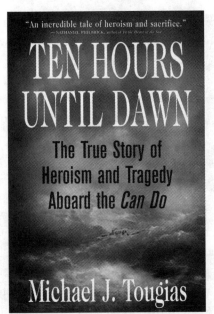

During the height of the Blizzard of 1978 the pilot boat Can Do, with five men onboard, set out from Gloucester to assist a lost Coast Guard boat and an oil tanker that was in a Mayday situation. *Ten Hours Until Dawn* tells the story of what happened on that awful night when the seas were producing monstrous waves of 40 feet and the wind was screaming at 100 miles per hour.

This is one of the few ocean tragedies where we know exactly what happened due to the existence of audio recordings which were taped the night of the storm and feature both the voices of men of the Coast Guard and the Can Do. The tapes span a ten hour period during the men's fight for survival.

"The best story of peril at sea since Sebastian Junger's Perfect Storm. Superb!" —Booklist

"What a story! Tougias' research and writing make the reader feel as if they are onboard the Can Do during the Blizzard of '78." —**Governor Michael Dukakis**

"An incredible tale of heroism and sacrifice." —**Nathaniel Philbrick, National Book Award Winner**

—Selected as an American Library Association Top Book of 2005

A Storm Too Soon:
The True Story of Disaster, Survival, and an Incredible Rescue

Seventy foot waves batter a tattered life raft 250 miles out to sea in one of the world's most dangerous places, the Gulf Stream. Hanging onto the raft are three men, a Canadian, a Brit, and their captain, JP DeLutz, a dual citizen of America and France. The waves repeatedly toss the men out of their tiny vessel, and JP, with 9 broken ribs, is hypothermic and on the verge of death. The captain, however, is a tough minded character, having survived a sadistic, physically abusive father during his boyhood, and now he's got to rely on those same inner resources to outlast the storm.

Trying to reach these survivors before it's too late are four Coast Guardsmen battling hurricane force winds in their Jayhawk helicopter. They know the waves in Gulf Stream will be extreme, but when they arrive they are astounded to find crashing seas of seventy feet, with some waves topping eighty feet. To lower the helicopter and then drop a rescue swimmer into such chaos is a high risk proposition. The pilots wonder if they have a realistic chance of saving the sailors clinging to the broken life raft, and if they will be able to retrieve their own rescue swimmer from the towering seas. Once they commit to the rescue, they find themselves in almost as much trouble as the survivors, facing several life and death decisions.

"By depicting the event from the perspective of both the rescued and the rescuers and focusing only on key moments and details, Tougias creates a suspenseful, tautly rendered story that leaves readers breathless but well-satisfied. Heart-pounding action for the avid armchair adventurer." —**Kirkus Review**

"Tougias deftly switches from heart-pounding details of the rescue to the personal stories of the boat's crew and those of the rescue team. The result is a well-researched and suspenseful read." —**Publishers Weekly**

"Few American authors—if any—can better evoke the realities that underlie a term such as 'desperate rescue attempt." —**Fall River Herald**

"Already a maven of maritime books with "Overboard!" and "Fatal Forecast", Tougias cinches that title here. Working in the present tense Tougias lets the story tell itself, and what a story! Any one reading (A Storm Too Soon) will laud Tougias' success." —**The Providence Journal**